More than Just a Girl

By

Irene Nndali Isiguzo

Published by:

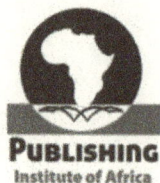

PUBLISHING
Institute of Africa

P. O. Box 16458-00100
Nairobi, Kenya.
info@publishing-institute.org
www.publishing-institute.org

ISBN: 978-9966-69-009-8

Contents

Dedicated to the African Girl-child, and to all those who have positioned themselves to ensure her spiritual, emotional and physical well being.

Acknowledgements

I sincerely appreciate my missionary family-my colleagues at Calvary Ministries International (CAPRO), partners, family & friends whom God used to not only encourage and support me but also to market the first edition of *More than Just a Girl*. God reward you all extravagantly!

Asante sana to my beautiful lanky daughter Lillian Otiego. You went through the draft when it was so raw no editor would touch it then!

I especially want to appreciate sister Grace Ayewah for the painstaking job of reading in-between the lines and for your professional input and for the inspiring foreword.

Many thanks to my brother, Elder Barine for your encouragement to see this through. May God reward your passion and dedication to excellence.

How do I thank the many teen girls God brought my way while I was a missionary in Kenya? Your stories and what God Almighty is able to do in your lives spurred me on to finish this book. May God the Potter reach out to you in His astounding grace and do in your lives what no man can do-giving you wings to fly!

My children Emeka, Shalom and David have continued to provide the ready laboratory where the principles in this book are daily being tried and tested. I cannot thank them enough for their many ideas and suggestions.

Chi, my rugged and rare hubby has continued to be a solid rock of unflinching support and encouragement. Thank you!

Foreword

More *than just a girl* is a must read for every teenager and a useful tool for guidance and counselling by parents, educators, the church and organizations interested in their well being. It is a well thought out material on sex education for the sincere seeker. It addresses truths and fallacies of self esteem faced by teenage girls as they begin to experience developmental changes from puberty to young adulthood.

Its timeliness cannot be overemphasized in our post-modern generation where the right values are relegated to the background and evil, celebrated. The language is simple and easy to read for any age. The style is lucid for the curious teenage girl with questions. The illustrations are apt and thought provoking. The technical elements are well researched and easy to comprehend. Parents and significant others who shy away from giving honest answers to teenage girls due to inhibitions induced by various cultures, have a ready guide in this book. This will help them freely initiate discussions that are capable of averting unwanted outcomes.

The author has taken the trouble to deal with issues like understanding the workings of hormones and the body make up, falling in love, abstinence, preparation for marriage and parent-child relationships with the right perspectives on life, without mincing words.

As a professional marriage counsellor now and former high school Guidance Counsellor, I endorse this book as a resource material for every library that cares about the girl child and her safe development. Any teenage girl who wants to soar high like an eagle and build her confidence in God must have a copy of this book in her personal library.

Grace Akpos Akpoarido Ayewah

M.Div. Pastoral, M.Ed. Counselling, B.Ed. History/English, PR.

Preface

One of the things I find exciting about God is He is that a storyteller. The Bible is God telling His story and that of His creation. This book is about our story yours and mine. These are the stories of the journey of young girls on their way to becoming grown women and the many roadblocks and pitfalls that they encounter. We truly and sincerely desire to be all that God our Maker designed us to be. However in our ignorance, foolishness and pride we trip, fall, make many blunders and our stories end 'happily never after'. But God Almighty is the Master story Rewriter. He takes a messed up story and rewrites it to fulfil His grand purpose and plan (Jeremiah 29:11). May this book point you towards the Master story Rewriter.

Introduction

Lara and her three cousins Folu, Shags and Remy had been secretly planning for an upcoming party with a quiet excitement. The D-day couldn't arrive early enough, but it finally did. As planned, all waited until the whole house was asleep. High-heeled shoes and other items had been smuggled out of the house earlier and hidden behind a nearby tree. When the coast was clear, Lara gave the signal. Then, one after the other, the 'Funky Four' as they jokingly referred to themselves, sneaked out of the house. They then tiptoed to the tree where they had hidden their clothes and other items.

Suddenly, as they picked up their stuff, a rough voice barked out in the dark, 'Hey who's there?' It was the neighbourhood night guard on patrol and right behind him the dogs! Startled and frightened out of their senses, Remy and Folu panicked and screamed. The sleeping house was rudely awakened with not-too-exciting results.

But things could get quite dangerous

Judy, a 16-year-old high school girl was found dead in a pool of blood in the school toilet. Investigations later revealed that she had had an abortion the previous day. A shadow of sadness descended and lingered over the entire school for a long time after the incident. A girl's life can be exciting and fun, but full of potential dangers.

Free to rock and roll!

Martha, a 17-year-old friend of mine said to me:

"There's a kind of excitement that seems to catch up with us girls, especially by the time we get to high school. A girl suddenly begins to kind of feel all grown-up and "ready-to-fly", you want to rock life but there are many obstacles."

"What are those obstacles?" I asked. She continued:

"A girl often feels like a prisoner looking out through a prison window into a garden with big and ripe tempting fruits. So, she eagerly awaits any opportunity to escape from the prison into that garden with all the waiting goodies! That is why we resent all the locks, chains, rules and curfews you adults come up with."

I could identify with her experience. I recall a time I wanted to escape from those intimidating locks, to attend a party. Thinking my aunt (whom my friends called Margaret Thatcher) was not in sight, I put on my favourite jeans and latest "killer" top, and was ready to go. As I was about to take that last step out of the gate into freedom, I heard her roar.

"Nnda-a-a-a-li! where do you think you are going?"

My adventure was over before it began. Like Martha you too may resent all the restrictions that parents and other authority figures often place over you. You may have wondered why parents and other authority figures tend to exercise more anxiety and strictness over girls, but not so much over boys.

You really want to know?

Here are the reasons:

1. Boys are not as vulnerable as girls.
2. It's easier to harm or abuse a girl than a boy.
3. Boys rarely get raped, never get pregnant or die from abortion.

4. Boys don't have wombs that could be damaged during rape or an abortion.

5. There's evidence that more teenage girls contract and die from HIV/Aids and other STDs (sexually transmitted diseases) than boys.

6. A young girl is the heart and mother of a nation- her very life, future and therefore her most precious possession. When we protect her, we protect a nation.

Dear girl

My goal in this book is to equip you with tried and true principles that will help you discover and joyfully fulfil your purpose in life. It is my prayer that it will inspire you to dare to become the person God truly made you to be −A PRINCESS!

I therefore urge you not to allow anyone or anything to place a limitation on you. God has placed the seeds of greatness inside of you; do not allow anything to hinder your journey to that greatness. Yes, your mother or the women you see around you may not inspire you to that greatness. Society may seem to place limitations on you and may often make you feel like you are nothing and that being a girl is a burden or even a curse. But you know what, as you will see through the pages of this book, no one can stop you. This is because God who made you is greater than any obstacles that may attempt to hold you back. You will soon discover that, you are more than just a girl−you are God's princess!

Dear Parent

This book is a response to the urgent need to help parents and guardians in their efforts to protect and rescue young girls from the traps and pitfalls of growing up. In every society, a girl is perceived as a potential wife and mother − the most influential person in any nation. Her responsibility it is to nurture and mould the life of not just her children but that of the entire society or nation. Thus the saying:

'Educate a boy, you educate an individual, educate a girl, you educate a nation.'

The devil is wicked and out to destroy. He recognizes the key role that girls play in God's overall plan for mankind. So his aim is to harm, destroy and hinder them from fulfilling God's purpose and destiny for their lives. But God has a great plan for every young girl no matter her circumstances and challenges. It is my prayer that parents and guardians will find this book helpful as they seek to partner with God to guide their girl or any girl under their influence into the wonderful future God has awaiting her.

More than Just a Girl

Chapter One

Girl with a Purpose

A girl's ultimate guide

A mobile phone is designed by the manufacturer to function in specific ways. The manufacturer then packages the mobile phone with a manual, which guides the owner on how to use the phone and get the best out of it. God is your great designer and manufacturer. The Bible is His word and your manual. In it you discover who you are, how you were designed, how you can function most effectively, and most of all, the purpose for which you were made.

My dear girl, I want you to realize that you are not an accident. God your maker knew beforehand that you would be a girl, what nation you would come from, your parents, your colour and what you would be and accomplish in life. If you must fulfil the purpose for which God made you, then you cannot ignore the Bible. He says in His Word that He knows the plans He has for you-they are good, to prosper and not harm you (Jeremiah 29:11). He is the one that formed you in your mother's womb (Psalm 139:13-16). He made you a girl to fulfil a purpose-never forget that.

God has a general purpose for His children.

● The Bible says He created us in His likeness. This means that as His children- He deposited His Spirit in us so that

17

we can be His ambassadors/representatives on this earth. Therefore the Spirit of God or the Holy Spirit is in us to reflect the character of God everywhere we go. This character is known as the fruit of the Spirit-love, joy, peace, patience, kindness, goodness, faithfulness, gentleness and self-control. As we submit to the Holy Spirit in obedience, He will enable us to resist the devil and live in a way that pleases and honours God.

● God wants us to be fruitful. He wants us to use the gifts that He has deposited in us to spread the plan of God for mankind all over the world. You don't need to travel all over the world to do this. Wherever you find yourself, tell others about the power of God and the love of Jesus. Let the light of Christ shine as you allow the Holy Spirit to reveal His fruit through your life. That way, others who are in the darkness of sin and power of Satan will gradually but surely come to the light.

● Ultimately God's purpose for all His children is to become like His son Jesus (Eph.4, Rom.8:29). What this means practically is that in my daily experiences as a girl, when issues confront me, I pause and consider, 'What is Jesus likely to do if He were in my shoes?'

If a guy were to pressure Him to indulge in premarital sex, what would be His response?

Would He cheat to pass exams?

Would He yield to peer pressure for fear of rejection?

Would He deceive His parents or lie to get out of trouble?

What would Jesus do?

When he was tempted he never yielded to sin. (Hebrews 4:15)

He never gave in to peer pressure. (John 7:3-10)

He forgave his enemies. (Luke 23:24)

His passion was to always please God. (John 4:34)

He never lost focus of his purpose. (Hebrews 12:2)

He cared for the needs of others. (Matthew 15:32)

Choosing to live like this doesn't come easy. However, once you recognize that there is the seed of greatness inside you because God made you in His likeness and you trust the Spirit of God to help you, you gradually discover that it isn't impossible. You can discover God's Special Purpose. Jeremiah, who was a young man, was told by God that he had been set apart by God from his mother's womb to be a prophet. Even through he felt inadequate, God encouraged him to rise up to the call to the nations of the world.

Mary was a young woman who had kept herself from engaging in premarital sex even after her engagement to Joseph. God chose her to be the mother of Christ the saviour of the world.

Florence Nightingale believed she heard the voice of God telling her that she had a special mission in life, though it was not clear what that mission was. At that time she wanted to study nursing but couldn't because it was not considered a suitable profession for a well-educated woman. Later, she volunteered at French Sisters of Charity as a nurse, where she focused on improving the health and living conditions of the soldiers. In 1860, she established Nightingale School for Nurses at St. Thomas's Hospital. It was the first school of its kind in the world. She is considered to be the founder of modern nursing.

A personal example

* I have always loved reading and writing. Many years ago while in the university, I felt God set me apart to write books that will touch and change lives.

What do you think God set you apart for? God will reveal it to you if you pray and pay attention.

How to discover your specific purpose

Through the gifts/talents God has endowed you with.

Joseph was gifted in the interpretation of dreams; this led to him becoming the Prime Minister of Egypt. God used this position to save the nation of Israel (Genesis 37–47). David the shepherd boy was a gifted composer and singer. God used this musical gift to bring him before the king (I Samuel16:17-23). Bezalel and Oholiab were chosen to beautify God's temple with their artistic gift (Exodus 31:1-11).

You may be very good in certain subjects when compared with other people, or have certain distinctive interests or hobbies. You may not be good in agriculture or art, but you could be very good in mathematics or physics. Your unique abilities can be a pointer to your purpose.

Certain life experiences can also be indicators of how God intends to use an individual in the future. Stormie Omartian, a young American woman was brought up by a mentally ill mother who made life very difficult for her. She ran away from home, attempted suicide, got involved in drugs, and went through other horrible experiences until she had an encounter with Jesus Christ. Through her difficult experiences, she learnt to draw close to God, study His Word and to pray. Today, she is a popular speaker and author of inspiring books on prayer.

Passion can also be a pointer to an individual's God-ordained purpose. As an example, you may have an unusual love for helping the poor, sick or the handicapped, or a strong love for plants and animals, or a strong hatred for a particular vice, such as prostitution or gambling and would do anything to rescue people from the hold of such destructive habits. These may be part of God's design to guide you into His unique purpose for your life.

A beauty queen discovers her purpose

"Oh my! What a lucky babe you are," Esther muttered to herself as she winked at her gorgeous image in the mirror. 'Life is so good,' she whispered again in front of her large wall length mirror, her huge eyes taking in the reflection of the golden bedroom. She turned away from the mirror, her high-heeled silver and diamond slippers digging into the thick golden Persian rug. She hummed a favourite tune. Her bedroom was her private paradise. The walls and ceilings were covered with oriental gold, ocean-blue and cream designs. The deep-red crisp brocade curtains were pulled aside and light streamed into the room, giving it a cheery sparkle. Her faithful maids, Tansha and Preket hovered around as they kept removing imaginary dust particles from the carpet and furniture. Esther's face beamed with an indulgent smile at her dear friends.

Esther strode towards the open window, took a deep breath, stomach in and chest out. She held that for a while then let out the air slowly. She did that several times. It was an exercise her uncle Mordecai had taught her. "It helps with relaxation and general well being," he had told her. She shook her head slightly. Uncle Mordi (as she fondly called him) was an interesting character. Esther was grateful to God for him. She turned to find Tansha behind her, curtsying as she said, "It is such a bright and beautiful day. Would you like to sit in your garden?"

"Oh Tansha, you are an angel," Esther replied as Tansha hurried out of the room.

It was every bit a fairy tale garden, with pink, red and white roses, ferns, lilies, daffodils and other breath-taking plants competing for attention. She was relaxed on her favourite garden chair as she cuddled her cat Laila. Her mobile phone rang, it was her uncle.

"Hello uncle Mordi, I was just thinking about you a while ago."

"Well, good thing you were, because all is not well," came the tense voice of uncle Mordecai. "What is it uncle? Is it your chest again? You sound bad," said Esther as she stood to her feet.

"No, it's our people. They are in trouble. That wicked Haman has paid 20 million dollars into the king's account as a reward for whoever can destroy our people."

"No! That's impossible." How do you know this? Oh my!"

"It doesn't matter. All over the country, our people, the Jews, are mourning. All my attempts to console them are in vain. You must arise and use your position to help. You must talk to the king."

"But how? What can I do? The king has not sent for me for some time. To go to him without an invitation means the death penalty, you know that. "

"Well, my dear young queen, you must realize that God did not put you in that palace just to enjoy yourself. He did it for a moment like this. You are at the crossroads. Remember Joseph who though was a slave became a Prime Minister? He discovered that He was made Prime Minister to save his people. Remember Deborah who also took great risks to save her people? It's now your turn."

"Uncle, what you are suggesting is scary, impossible, but I'll see what I can do, I'll call you back."

Esther sat down with a faraway look on her face, her brows creased by a frown.

"This is unbelievable! How can anyone do this? We are such a peace-loving, hard-working people. What should I do? I don't want to die. God has blessed me and I don't want to lose all these." Her huge confused eyes moved slowly over the huge palace courtyard.

"Oh God, help me, I want to be like Deborah, and Joseph, but I'm afraid to die. She buried her face in her laps and sobbed quietly. Finally Esther raised her head, her eyes red and face wet with tears. With a determined glint in her eyes, she knew what she must do. She dialled her uncle's number."

"Yes uncle, it's okay. Please gather all our people. Let everyone fast for three days – no food or water. My maids and I will do the same. After that, I'll go to the king and if I die, so be it."

The story of Queen Esther did not end here. You can read the full account in the book of Esther in the Bible. She did not die. God honoured her faith and courage. With the help of God she was able to use her position and influence to save her people. Even though making the choice at the crossroads was difficult and risky, Esther did not shy away from it. Her uncle Mordecai helped her realize her purpose. She was not a beauty queen just to show off or to feel better than other girls. She was born to use the gift and privileges God had given her to help and save others. Her uncle helped her discover her purpose.

Note: *The biblical story of Esther has been paraphrased and adapted to reflect the modern times in which we live in.*

Discussion Questions

1. If you desire to fulfil God's purpose for your life, what must you not ignore? Why?

2. What do you believe is God's purpose for your life generally and specifically?

3. What are the things in your life God can use to guide you into His specific purpose for you?

4. How did Queen Esther discover God's specific purpose for her life?

5. What principles can you learn from Esther's life as you seek to know God's purpose for your own life?

6. How can you distinguish between a girl who lives a life of purpose and one who does not?

7. Why do you think many girls live a life without purpose?

8. Who gave Esther the courage to risk her life to save her people?

9. Memorise Proverbs 29:18 and Daniel 11:32.

Chapter Two

Of Eagles and Chickens

There was once a farmer who raised chicken. One day while out in the forest he found a large egg. He wondered what animal had laid it and took it home to see if one of his chickens would hatch it. He put the egg under one of his hens who was sitting on her own eggs at the time. With time her eggs which were smaller in size began to hatch. The larger new egg however hatched last. Then out of it crawled a larger chicken with big feet and a greyish colour. The other chicks avoided it, not only because it was larger but it behaved unlike them in many ways. The bigger bird felt rejected and isolated.

One day while looking up at the sky he noticed two graceful magnificent birds soaring high in the sky. The sound they made, unlike that of the chickens were attractive to his ears. He felt like they were calling him. They seemed to say, *'come fly with us'*. From then on he began to think only of flying. But he reasoned that chickens don't fly, they are not heavenly like those majestic birds.

One day when no one was looking, he suddenly flapped his wings and to his surprise he found himself rise off the ground gracefully and powerfully. But he was too afraid to fly, after all chickens don't fly. And besides, what will the other chickens say? But he secretly continued to dream about flying. Those majestic birds would return from time to time, soaring above the sky and calling to him to go fly with them.

One day he suddenly flapped his wings and up he flew into the sky to meet those other birds. However, as he flew closer, he found that they looked just like him. Suddenly it dawned on him, *'I am an eagle, and not a chicken'*. His joy knew no bounds as he realized he was where he belonged.

They asked him why it took him so long to join them. He replied, *'I was born among chickens and lived among them; I thought I was a chicken.'*

The senior eagle replied, *'You acted like a chicken because you thought like a chicken, but now that you know the truth, it has set you free to be what you were created to be and do-* **to soar.***'*

Who am I?

Before you can begin to fulfil God's purpose for your life, you must recognize who you truly are. Who you are is not what others say about you or even what you think or how you feel about yourself. Your mum, dad or others may have called you a stupid or hopeless girl. Your mates may say you are weird and your teachers might have concluded that you are a mistake or a failure. You might have been told again and again you will not make it in life. The sad thing is, you feel stupid and have come to think they all must be right. What I want you to realize is that what they say, what you feel or presently think does not matter, what matters is what God says about you.

I want you hence- forth to begin to think and believe only what God says about you in His Word, the Bible. **Confess what the Bible says about you:**

● I am a child of God (John 1:12).

● I am the light of the world (Matthew 5:14).

- I am an ambassador of Christ (2 Corinthians 5:10).

- I am Christ's friend (John 15:15).

- I am God's dwelling place-His temple (1 Cor. 3:16, 1Cor. 6:19).

- I am a joint-heir with Christ-I share His inheritance (Romans 8:17).

- I am more than a conqueror (Romans 8:37).

- I am priceless-more costly than rubies (Proverbs 31).

- I am the head and not the tail (Deuteronomy 28:13).

- I am chosen, called of God (1Peter 2:9).

- I am blessed (Ephesians 1:3).

In addition to all these, the Bible says you are an **eagle.** The eagle is a unique and special bird. So special that the Bible describes God as an eagle. The children of God are also described as eagles. (Deuteronomy 32:11-12, Isaiah 40:31.) People who trust God and rely on Him become like the eagle. Most girls have no idea they were born to be eagles, (because they don't read the Bible) so they live like chickens. A timid, stupid, ignorant and weak person is usually described as a chicken. Chickens have wings, but can't fly. Chickens are not selective about what they feed on or where they go. They are forever pecking amongst garbage dumps, for worms, rotten, smelly and dead stuff. Chickens are earthly and ordinary. But eagles are not like that. Eagles are quite different. They are majestic and heavenly.

What makes the Eagle special?

1. The Eagle's build:
The eagle is larger in size, has a more powerful build with a heavier head and beak than other birds. The beak is very

large and hooked for tearing flesh from its prey. It can also hit a prey with the force of a bullet. It has strong muscular legs and powerful talons which enables it to grasp its prey with an iron-grip. How does this apply to you as a teen?

You may be small in size, young in age, weak in many areas, but if you begin to believe what the Bible says about you, you can become a giant eagle. Though David was just a teen-ager, his faith made him bigger than Goliath, and he killed the giant (I Samuel 17:43-50). You are as big as what you believe, therefore make sure you believe the truth and not lies. Believing lies will make you a victim.

2. Wings

The eagles' wings are superior to the wings of other birds. They are longer and more evenly broader than those of other birds. Therefore they fly faster, higher and longer. Hardly do eagles perch on the ground or small trees. They live at very high altitudes. They soar high in the sky, they are heavenly birds. They build their nests on tall trees, high cliffs and on the clefts of rocky mountains. Even though this is a very difficult task, the eagle is determined and pursues it to the finish. Why? They realize that at this high peak, they and their young ones are secure from predators.

3. They are Fearless

Due to the superiority of their wings; eagles don't avoid storms but are able to soar above them in troublesome weather.

How does this apply to you?

It is all about foundations. Have you built your own life on Christ the Solid Rock? Or are you taking the easy way out? Are you building your life on what you see others building, such as fashion, pleasure, fun, food, etc? If you build your life on anything but Christ, sooner or later you will crash like Humpty-Dumpty who had a great fall and his broken pieces could not be put together.

How can you receive eagle wings?

- To receive your wings you must give your heart and entire life to Christ.

- When you ask Him, Christ will forgive your sins and cleanse your heart with His blood. The Bible says, '*all have sinned and come short of the glory of God.*' (Romans 3:23)

- Christ will come into your heart and give you power to live supernaturally. '*As many as received Him to them gave He the power to become the sons of God...*' (John 1:12)

When you receive Christ into your heart, you receive the grace and power to live an extraordinary life. Receiving Christ into your heart makes you a carrier of Jesus wherever you go. This not only gives you confidence and boldness, it also opens you up to God's blessings- answered prayer, protection, guidance, peace, joy and finally heaven (2 Peter 1:3-4, 1 Peter 2:9).

Just like Clark Kent removes his ordinary clothes to reveal his superman suit underneath, you too can throw away the negative labels others have attached to you, to reveal the real you underneath. The real eagle designed by God, with supernatural wings and abilities to do anything and to soar above any obstacle. You can confront and overcome all the stuff that defeats other teens e.g. Peer pressure, pre-marital sex, low-self esteem, ungodly music, poverty, lying, cheating, rebellion, alcohol, stealing, drugs, etc. It's an exciting life full of incredible possibilities! The sky is just the beginning!

Here's the next thing that sets the eagle apart:

4. Vision

The eagle has extremely large pupils, which makes its sight eight times better than that of man and no bird has sight comparable to it. It can sight its food from far off and dive for it. Also, it can see danger a long way off and avoid it. It's hard to surprise, fool or trap the eagle because of its far-off vision. God wants you to have the excellent vision of an eagle. Some people have eyes but no vision. <u>People with eagle -vision see far into the future</u>. They dream dreams of what they desire for their future. They imagine what their future could be and they plan and prepare themselves for that bright and better tomorrow.

Imagine that you want to be a role model in the field of medicine, law, preaching the Bible, sports, banking and finance, education, or music. So you plan by prayer, hard work, seeking godly advice and writing down the ideas that come to your mind. What do you do when temptations come? You remember your vision /dream and you quickly run from the temptations. Because you know that sex before marriage, abortion, drugs, alcohol or lesbianism can steal your vision and future. Vision will help you see that the friends you keep, books you read, movies you watch, habits, acts you partake in and places you go could affect your life in the future. And above all determine where you will spend your future when you die- heaven or hell.

How do you get the eagle-vision?

● First, by receiving your special wings, as earlier mentioned.

● Then by prayer, reading and letting the Word of God be your guide in daily decisions and regularly seek godly advice.

● Write down your dreams for the future – keep the notebook safe.

● Cut out pictures of people who inspire you and paste in your notebook.

● Also collect quotes, stories, songs and poems that inspire you.

● Write Bible verses and characters that touch your heart in it too. Whenever you relax, you are discouraged or tempted, go through the notebook and pray- it will keep you focused on your future.

● Study and work hard, develop your gifts and talents.

'I …pray also that the eyes of your heart be enlightened in order that you may know the hope to which He has called you…'(Eph. 1:17)

'Your word is a lamp to my feet and a light for my path.' (Ps. 119:105)

5. Diet

The popular saying, *'you are what you eat'* is true. You are not just what you eat but you are as strong as what you eat. The eagle is very particular about its food. Unlike chickens and other birds, the eagle never eats dead food. Usually it would hunt and catch a live chicken or fish from a river for its meal. No wonder it has the greatest life span amongst birds-Some eagles can live as long as 80 to 100 years (compare that with the average life span of an African male- about 47 years).

Like the eagle you **must discipline yourself to hunt for rich, nourishing and living food.** What is living food?

Living Food = the Word of God

One day I was travelling in a public transport, and sitting opposite me was a cool girl reading her Bible. Most girls will not even let others know they read their Bibles, let alone reading it in a public place. They would rather read popular comics, fashion/glamour magazines and secular novels. They believe this shows they are cool big girls. They are afraid of being mocked by their peers. That shows such girls are chickens. But once you allow Christ into your life and you mean business with Him, He will give you power to be bold and courageous.

You must make up your mind to do like the eagle- HUNT for your food. You hunt for something out of reach-you look for it, pursue, search for, chase, and seek for it. This calls for effort- *determination, perseverance, patience* and *aggressiveness.* Just as you find time to read fashion magazines, talk to your friends on phone, watch TV, surf the internet, etc. You must find time to read your Bible and talk to God. Because the devil knows that the Word of God will bring miracles and great blessings into your life, he will do all he can to keep you from it. He will convince you it's boring, difficult to understand, old-fashioned, etc. But the devil is a liar. The Word of God is the number one best–seller of all time.

Why should you pay attention to God's Word?

"Your word I have treasured in my heart, that I may not sin against You" (Psalm 119:11).

"Your word is a lamp to my feet and a light to my path" (Psalm 119:105).

"This book of the law shall not depart from your mouth, but you shall meditate on it day and night, so that you may be careful to do according to all that is written in it; for then you will make your way prosperous, and then you will have success" (Joshua 1:8).

"The unfolding of your words gives light; It gives understanding to the simple" (Psalm 119:130).

"Blessed are those who hear the word of God and observe it." (Luke 11:28).

Inasmuch as you find time to read fashion magazines, talk to your friends on phone, chat on social media, watch TV, surf the internet, and do the myriads of other things girls occupy their time with, you should find time to regularly read your Bible so that you can reap the benefits outlined above.

Other living food

● Books/literature that inspire you to excel, succeed, build your character, develop your gifts, talents and broaden your knowledge of the world far and near.

- Music that inspires you to worship God, be responsible, have clean fun, etc.

- Movies that entertain in a clean way, and also inspire and teach positive values and morals.

Dead food

- Pornography-books/magazines and movies that show nakedness and sexual activities.

- Romance books that arouse you sexually.

- Movies and soap operas that promote sex before marriage, adultery, sexual scenes etc.

- Unhealthy hip-hop, rock music with lyrics about sex outside marriage, violence, etc.

Such foods are rotten and smelly, meant only for the garbage dump. They are chicken food; they will poison and render your life purposeless.

Finally the eagle is special because of:

6. The Eagles Association!

The eagle does not move with the crowd. Eagles fly higher and faster and live at very high altitudes. They are more focused and live on a different diet from other birds. Therefore they do not flock together with lesser birds. To be an eagle, you must recognize that you are different, and so be prepared not to go with the crowd if their lifestyle is contrary to that of an eagle. Throughout this book you will find principles that will empower you to be an eagle. If you dare to apply them, these principles will lift you out of the crowd and make you a pacesetter or role model. Prepare to stand alone if necessary. Recognize that you are an eagle, not a chicken, so live like one!

Discussion Questions

1. Would you currently describe yourself as an eagle or a chicken? Explain your answer.

2. What makes the eagle different from chickens and other birds?

3. Why do so many girls live like a chicken?

4. What do you understand by the phrase "dead food"?

5. Why do many girls prefer "dead food" to "living food"?

6. What do eagles feed on? What do eagles never eat?

7. How can you develop eagle vision?

8. How would you ensure that as an eagle you don't reduce yourself or allow anyone to reduce you to a chicken?

9. Memorise Isaiah 40:29-31.

Chapter Three

She is groovy!

In order to fulfil your purpose, God designed and gave you a unique and wonderful body. The teen years being discussed in this book are often described as the adolescent phase. During this adolescent phase, (for girls between 8 and 13, boys between 9 and 14) so many changes are going on within the adolescent/teen girl. These changes are not just physical, but also biological and emotional.

The good news however, is that the changes are a signal that a girl is about to transform into a woman. There's a biological clock in every girl (boys too!). As this clock ticks away, time and nature gradually, but surely move you forward towards womanhood.

Though these changes occur in the body, they also affect the mind and emotions. So a girl may wake up in the morning thinking and feeling great about herself. You could say, she feels 'high'. She dances, sings her way through her chores and the day. But the next day she wakes up feeling low and thinking life is just too much. She reacts rudely to her mom, won't do her chores, finds homework overwhelming. She may storm out of the kitchen, collapse on her bed sobbing at something her mum said. However, during dinnertime she is okay, humming the latest tunes. No wonder adults often feel teens are from another planet!

Stages of sexual development

The truth is, sexual development begins in the womb. A baby girl is born with thousands of immature ova or eggs in her ovaries. By age 8, behind the scenes, hormonal changes begin. Oestrogen, the most important female hormone, begins to be produced by the ovaries. This happens when the brain tells the pituitary gland to begin to produce follicle-stimulating hormone (FSH) that then stimulates the ovaries to make oestrogen.

Stage 1-(Between 8 & 11 years) Ovaries enlarge, hormone production begins, but no external visible development yet.

Stage 2-(Between 8 & 14 years) 1st external sign is breast development. Breast buds form nipples, which are tender and elevated. The area around the nipple increases in size. 1st pubic hair appears in the pubic area/ vulva (onset of puberty), body weight and height increase. Body becomes rounder and curvier. The skin changes and it glows.

Stage 3-(Between 9 & 15years) Breast development continues. Pubic hair becomes coarser and darker and hair may grow on legs. If you decide to shave the hairs, be sure to use clean water and a new razor. Never use a razor that another person has used. This is to avoid infection. The waist gets smaller and the hips wider. More fat gets deposited in the stomach and buttocks- no need to fear that you are becoming fat, it's a sign you are developing into a woman. A whitish discharge from the vagina may appear; a sign the vagina is self-cleansing. Menses may begin. Skin glows, voice becomes more melodious.

Stage 4-(Between 10 &16 years) In some girls, the area around the nipple becomes even darker, and separates into a little mound rising above the rest of the breast. Pubic hair increases and menses begin if they didn't at stage 3. Ovulation may begin but may not be regular. Periods can be regular even if ovulation is not. Note that there can be menses without ovulation.

Stage 5-(Between 12 &19 years) The final stage. By now most girls reach their full height. Ovulation is now regular, breasts are fully developed and pubic hair is full.

A closer look at this great body undergoing transformation:

The area in-between a girl's legs is usually called the vagina, but this is not totally true. In-between your legs is the vulva, made up of two small pear shaped sets of lips (the labia major and labia minora).

1. The labia majora (or big lips, which protect the rest of the vagina, and as a girl matures is covered by pubic hair.)

2. The labia minora (or small lips, under the big lips. These vary in colour, size and shape. Have no fat or padding. They are made up of blood vessels, oil and scent glands.)

3. The clitoris- It lies at the point where the big and small lips connect. It is small but sensitive.

4. The urethra- The urine opening, lies below the clitoris.

5. Vaginal opening-connects the inner and outer genitalia. The real vagina is the moist, long canal that stretches from the vaginal opening to the back of the vagina.

6. The cervix- Lies at the back of the vagina and is dimple-shaped.

7. Uterus-small, pear shaped and made up mostly of muscle tissue. It can expand quite a lot during pregnancy.

8. Fallopian tubes-are above the uterus, they are passages from the uterus to the ovaries.

9. Ovaries- where eggs are stored.

Preparing for your first period:

This may happen between 10 and 16 years but the average is between 12 and 14.

* Don't be caught unawares. Look forward to your first menses – it is a good sign that one of these days, you will become a mother.

- It will be good to buy some sanitary pads and keep with you – there are small sizes for young ladies of every age. If you cannot afford towels from the shops, an old but washed and clean cloth can be cut into small pieces to fit into your panties.

- If you have not started your menses yet and your mum has not yet talked to you about it, ask her. It is nothing to be shy or ashamed about; it is a beautiful experience. You can ask any trustworthy woman around you about it.

- Suppose you suddenly spot blood on your panties while in school or away from home? Do not panic, if you are in school tell your (female) teacher. Or if away from home, just get into a store, buy some pads and go to a public toilet and place the pad on your panties. You can find a lady to help you.

Note these points

- Cleanliness – A girl's body is open, which means foreign bodies/germs, etc. can easily get in and cause an infection, which can be quite serious. Therefore make sure you use clean pads and panties. Don't use another's panties. Don't keep your pads exposed – e.g. lying on the bed, on chairs or dump them in your suitcase. Keep them covered in a clean container/bag.

- Bath at least twice a day during your menses or you will smell. Blood is made up of mostly proteins, therefore just like beans and meat it has the tendency to attract bacteria and cause a disgusting odour. Perfumes and deodorant can help, but must not replace the bath!

- Menses may be quite painful for some girls- serious and prolonged abdominal pain, nausea, dizziness and in some, vomiting. Sometimes it may be serious enough to see a doctor. There is no cause for alarm if these occur.

People are different and so react differently to the bodily changes mentioned. You may need pain relievers.

● Note however that your attitude, the way you see your period matters a lot. If you think negatively about it, as if it is a curse or a headache, you are more likely to have painful and unpleasant periods. But if you think of it as a blessing and gift from God, you are more likely to feel better when it occurs.

● Other signs you may note when your menses approach are breast enlargement and painfulness. Headache, migraine, increased heart-beat, fatigue, abdominal, leg and lower back cramps and bloating (gas in the stomach). Some pimples on the face or exceptionally smooth skin – a form of beauty that makes boys seem more attracted to a girl than usual. This calls for self-control and discipline, so don't let that get into your head. The hormones released during the menses affect a girl's emotions as well. One time she's all high and excited, the next she's depressed and anxious. Sometimes you may think you are abnormal or going crazy! This is very tricky, but don't let that disturb you for it comes and goes like the waves of the sea!

● At first – your menses may come after every 2 months – but gradually they do normalize. This is because your hormones are building up – i.e. the female hormones oestrogen and progesterone. By the time they fully build up, you will see your menses once in a month. It usually lasts between 3 – 5 days, in some cases up to seven days.

● If you are not having sex and you miss your period, you don't need to be alarmed, this can happen under certain circumstances.

● However, if your period was regular and suddenly becomes irregular, then you <u>may need to see a doctor</u>, just to ensure that things are ok. Often there is no cause for alarm- it could be as a result of stress, low iron in the body or general poor nutrition. <u>Other reasons to see a doctor include:</u>

● Excessively heavy bleeding -if you are soaked and need to change within an hour.

● Extremely light bleeding-at first it should be light, but after it normalizes it should flow properly.

● If by age 15 a girl has not started her menses-again there is often no need to be alarmed, because we all differ.

<u>Cultural consideration:</u> Menses are not a curse or taboo. It's a normal biological process and there is nothing to be ashamed of. Though it is good to be aware of how your culture views it, don't let anyone use it to intimidate or embarrass you. In the African culture, men are often embarrassed by talk about menses. They call it 'woman sickness'. If you need to collect money from a male relative who you live with to buy sanitary pads, and they insist on what you need it for, calmly and without shame say it's for your menses. But it's not wise to discuss details of your body functions with a male; it can cause unnecessary closeness leading to sexual intimacy.

What can you do to minimize the discomforts of menses?

● Develop a positive attitude about your menses -for example as it approaches pray '*Lord thank you for making me a woman, help me to enjoy my womanhood including my menses.*'
● Study your body, how you feel and what you observe before and after each month.
● Try writing down your observations, experiences and feelings if you can. Especially, keep a record of your menses, when it starts and ends. It would be very important information when you need to see a doctor and when you get married and you need to begin to plan to have babies.

Improve your diet- eat more natural foods (green leafy vegetables, whole grains, tubers, cereals, fruits,) etc. than processed foods like cakes, sweets and carbonated drinks (sodas). Avoid milk and sugar, reduce salt, fats, red meat, and drink plenty of water. Avoid alcohol. Avoid lying down all day when you have your menses, it hinders blood flow. Exercise is necessary-stretch, jump, skip, swim, run, dance, etc.

Great, but watch out!

Your menses occur because about every 28 days the uterus prepares itself to receive the egg, which if fertilized by a man's sperm would become a baby. However, when this does not happen, the inner layer of the uterus, which has been prepared to carry a baby, is no longer needed. Therefore this layer is shed from the body and flows out as blood, this is known as menses or period. So it's like the womb 'weeps' and sheds 'tears of blood' because it has no baby to carry.

What does this mean?

● That once you begin your menses you can become pregnant if you have sex with a man/boy.

● You can get pregnant without penetration - if you let a man play with your private parts such that he 'accidentally' pours sperm from his penis near your vagina.

How is this possible?

Can a girl become pregnant without a man putting his penis into her vagina?
This is possible because as the man plays with your genitals, or as you touch his penis he can ejaculate outside the vagina without you knowing. This ejaculation releases millions of sperm in fluid form (about 200 million) and some can swim

down your thighs into the vagina without your knowledge. From there, one sperm can penetrate the fallopian tube and fertilize an egg that has been released from the ovary. So don't allow any guy deceive you with *"don't worry, you won't get pregnant, I will be careful, I won't go in."*

Masturbation

About seven days after your menses, your ovaries will release eggs – this is known as ovulation. This is the period a girl's sex-drive is strongest. Most girls would feel sexually excited and often this is when many begin **masturbation** – i.e. using their fingers or any other object to rub on their private part, until they feel intense and pleasurable sexual release. Some girls go as far as putting hard long objects inside their vagina. Often masturbation is a sign that a girl is sad, lonely, insecure, etc. So masturbation becomes a way of escape from her miseries. Many teens get addicted to it and it controls them. Anything that controls you is your master and you the slave. But through the name of Christ any bondage can be broken. '*If the son of man (Christ) sets you free, you are free indeed.*' (Galatians 5:1). Masturbation is like having sex with yourself, which is not Biblical. Sex is for a man and a woman in marriage (more on this later). There was the case of a girl who was using unripe plantain to masturbate and it broke in her vagina. Lack of self-control is harmful. If you are already hooked to masturbation, you can stop. Share with a trusted, mature and godly friend, teacher (female!) or woman-who can advice and pray with you.

It's not 'love' but hormones!

Also during ovulation, a girl feels a need to be closer to a boy than usual. She may also feel like being kissed or having sex. This makes most teens think they are in love if a guy shows interest in them at this time. This is a very tricky period, which calls for determination and discipline. These feelings come and go because more sex hormones are released during the ovulation period. This occurs about 15 days from the day you see your menses. But after ovulation the hormones decrease, and the feelings pass. This is why teens fall in and out of love. A girl who has chosen to keep herself pure will not yield to these temporary sexual urges no matter the pressure.

One thing you must learn from the onset is that sexual feelings are not wrong, but the challenge is how to respond to them. <u>So self-control is very important.</u>

How do I handle the sexual urge?

Sexual feelings are controllable. They are natural feelings created by God and they occur at certain seasons. It is a natural feeling to alert you that if you were married and you had sex with your husband at this time of ovulation, you could become pregnant. If you are not yet married, this feeling is not meant to be satisfied but controlled for the short time it lasts. If I get hungry while in a shopping mall, will I because of hunger break into the snack bar and steal a chicken pie? Eagles don't live by convenience, but by their conscience.

One wise step is to avoid going to a secluded place when the desire to masturbate comes. Avoid places and activities that will worsen the sexual temptation, e.g. watching a sensual movie, listening to sensual music or visiting that boy that has been hitting on you.

Find something to do, e.g. wash, sweep, or take a walk. Don't be on your own. Call a godly friend, pray, memorize a verse to say at this time. For example:

1. 'My body is the temple of the Holy Spirit (1Cor. 6:19)'.

2. 'Christ has set us free, stand firm then, and do not … be burdened again by a yoke of slavery (Gal. 5:1)'.

With eagle determination and God's help, you can make it.

Discussion Questions

1. What is adolescence?

2. What is sex-drive and what does the Bible say about it?

3. What are hormones and how do they affect the development of the teenage girl?

4. How can a young girl prepare for her first menstrual period?

5. What are the signs you may likely observe at the approach of and during your menses?

6. What should you watch out for as regards sexual feelings and relationship with the opposite sex?

7. How should you handle sexual urges during your cycle?

8. Memorise Philippians 4:13 and I Corinthians 6:12. Discuss how these verses can be applied to a teenage girl's life.

Chapter Four

Don't be silly; be sensible!

Comfort and Trina had been close since they were five-years-old. When they finished primary school they got admission into the same boarding school. It was there that Comfort began to hang out with girls and boys she considered cool and trendy. Her closeness to Trina gradually cooled off. But as her closeness with this 'cool' group grew, she got more and more into trouble. Trina however refused to let go. She would visit as usual, give advice and comfort when necessary. One night Comfort and three other girls sneaked out of the hostel to attend a party. At the party there was an incident; some girls were drugged and raped. Comfort was one of them. She was in hospital for a week. Trina wept for her friend. She kept awake at night to copy notes for Comfort in the various subjects. She visited her at home after she was discharged. They held each other tight. Both were in tears.

A true friend is a gift from God

One of the best choices a girl can make is to develop healthy friendships with other girls. A healthy friendship is that which enables or inspires you to develop godly character and also to achieve your goals and dreams. It is a friendship that is characterized by honesty, loyalty, integrity, moral purity, mutual respect, self-discipline, and dependability-qualities found in eagle girls.

An unhealthy friendship is characterized by the opposite- dishonesty, disloyalty, immorality, indiscipline, etc. In such a friendship you or your friend will influence each other into activities/ habits that corrupt your character and hinder you from achieving your goals and dreams. Such a friendship reduces you to a chicken.

Who is a friend?

A true friend;

- Desires and seeks your good and happiness.
- Loves you for yourself. Not for your looks or what she/he can get from you.
- Will not gossip about you, but will tell you the truth even if it hurts.
- Is someone you can trust because she is not a pretender.
- Respects your views and beliefs.
- Will not force you to do what you believe is wrong.
- Will not encourage you to disobey your parents/constituted authority.
- Will rejoice when you succeed, and cry with you when you hurt.
- Will support/encourage you to achieve your dreams/goals.

To have a healthy friendship, you must determine to seek out eagle girls (and boys). As the common saying goes, Birds of a feather flock together, which means that similar people tend to associate with each other.

Attempt this exercise

1. List ten qualities you believe eagle girls should possess.
2. How many do you and your friends possess?
3. How would you describe you and your friends- eagles or chickens?
4. How can you acquire these qualities?
5. When will you begin?

Here are some eagle qualities:

- They recognize their identity as daughters of the King of kings.

- They set the pace rather than follow the crowd.

- They follow their conscience even when it is hard.

Does choosing to make friends with only eagle girls mean you are proud? Not at all. Birds of the same feather flock together. The word of God says, *'He who walks with the wise grows wise, but a companion of fools suffers harm'*. (Proverbs 13:20).

'Do not be misled, bad company corrupts good character'. (1 Corinthians15:33.) This means that if you hang out with eagles (the wise), sooner or later, you will become like them. If however you walk with fools (chickens), you will end up a fool in the end. As a new girl in town, Dinah the beautiful daughter of Jacob was not careful about choosing her friends. Such a careless attitude led to her being at the wrong place at the wrong time, consequently she was raped (Genesis 34:1-2). The Bible commands young people to refuse negative influences but seek out godly ones.

'My son if sinners entice you, do not give in to them…..do not go along with them…' (Prov. 1:10- 15).

If you are not an eagle yet, you can become one right now. It's as simple as ABC.

A- Accept that you are a sinner (according to the Bible, *'all have sinned and come short of the glory of God'* Romans 3:23).

B- Believe in your heart that Christ died for your sins and rose again from the dead.

C- Confess that Jesus died for your sins and rose again from the dead.

'If you confess with your mouth, Jesus is Lord' and believe in your heart that that God raised Him from the dead, you will be saved' (Romans 10:9).
You can also go back to chapter 2 for more details.

Even though friends are very important in our lives, we must beware of negative peer pressure.

Negative peer pressure (NPP)

Para, a tall, slim and chocolate-skinned 15-year-old beauty, received Christ into her life in her second year in high school. Her total transformation and bubbly joy motivated her alcoholic single mum to do the same. She was a leader in the school fellowship and also one of the top performers in school. But two years later, a notorious bully called Moo-moo began to harass her. She began to feel intimidated by her non born-again friends. They mocked her commitment and lifestyle. They teased her about taking religion too far and that she will one day regret for not enjoying her youth, etc. At first she ignored them, but soon she began to feel they were right. And one day she blurted out, "I'm tired of this 'Jesus stuff.'" She quit the Christian fellowship and joined the fun-chasers club. After a while she became pregnant and dropped out of school to have her baby. Because of shame she had to change schools. It took months of counselling from her mum and pastor to get her out of depression and onto her feet again. Have you guessed who this notorious Moo-moo is? Moo-moo is none other than what you have always known as peer pressure.

What is peer pressure?

Moo-moo means stupid or zombie. Stupid means unintelligent, slow, dull, dim-witted, brainless, etc. Stupid also means unwise, foolish, silly, daft, pitiful, ridiculous, etc. A stupid person cannot think correctly, therefore is unable to make correct choices. A zombie/robot is a machine that is incapable of having its own thoughts. It has to be controlled before it can function. Chickens are like that. Therefore to yield to negative peer pressure –NPP (we shall soon see the positive side) is to admit that you are stupid, silly, and brainless and cannot think for yourself. To yield to NPP is to follow the crowd. It means you have no mind of your own. Chickens are pressure-driven, but eagles are purpose-driven. When you yield to peer pressure you are saying that you would rather obey your peers than God or your own intelligence. And you would rather offend God than your peers. But this is the height of foolishness. As a result of peer-pressure, some girls have died from abortion, been raped, gotten into drugs ended up psychiatric cases, etc. The Bible strongly warns against the folly of disobeying God in order to please a friend, family member, etc. The Bible clearly instructs you to oppose and resist anyone who entices you to disobey God. Such a person is guilty and is liable to face the death penalty. (Deuteronomy 13:6).

Self-image and peer pressure

What is self-image? Self-image is the inward opinion you have of yourself. It is the way you see and evaluate yourself; it is your self-worth or self- esteem. This is extremely important, because you are controlled by the way you see yourself. If you have a positive self-image, your self-esteem is high. No matter your circumstances you position yourself to be happy and successful. Often, teens have a low opinion of themselves. A girl may see herself as 'too fat', 'thin as a broomstick', 'shapeless', 'dull', 'worthless', etc. Usually these evaluations are wrong, because they are based on other people's opinions, mainly that of your peers. If you recognize that you are made in the image of God, that He is your father and has a purpose for your life, no matter the faults you may have, your self-image will be positive. In that case you will not likely yield to peer-pressure, because you know who you are and where you are going in life. But if you see yourself as 'stupid' or 'nothing' your self-image will be poor, you will feel worthless, think, act and live like a stupid girl or a chicken. You will do anything to make others notice, like and accept you. Therefore you will more likely yield to negative peer pressure.

The main reason teen girls have sex outside marriage is because of negative peer pressure or poor self-image. A girl with a poor self image is desperate for approval, love and acceptance. So if any guy comes around and says 'I love you' (which for most guys means I want to have sex with you), such a girl will likely give in because she longs for someone to hold her and make her feel special. She does not mind losing her virginity if it will draw a guy close to her and also make her accepted by her peers. Such a girl is a chicken, will take any insult from a guy, and will allow people to treat her like trash. But if a girl sees herself as a daughter of God Almighty, a princess, she will not cheapen herself before guys or let people treat her carelessly. Such a girl is usually confident and focused and not easily intimidated. She recognizes that she is an eagle and she lives like one. Such girls with a positive self-image are usually pace-setters. Wherever they are they stand out as role-models.

To boost your self-image:

● Daily look at and point to yourself in the mirror and say to your image,
'Irene (say your own name) you are the daughter of the King of kings, you are a princess, an eagle, God's temple, light of the world, a winner, an ambassador of heaven, fearfully and wonderfully made, the head and not the tail, …' etc.

● When you make a mistake, don't say *'oh no I never get things right'*, say *'oh well, it's okay, I will keep at it until I get it right'*. *'I can do all things through Christ.'*

● When people criticize you, even if it is done unkindly, take it positively and quickly find the truth in what they say and apply it in your life. E.g. If it's true that you are lazy, untidy, performing academically poor, etc. pray and ask God to help you make the necessary changes.

● Avoid self-pity, self-hatred, self-defence and self-justification, rather pursue self-discipline and self-correction. If you do so, you are on your way to becoming a star-an eagle.

Let's see how a positive self-mage affects you (the cool side of peer pressure!)

POSITIVE PEER PRESSURE (PPP)

The Saving Arrows

Mandy, Henrietta, Carol and Daisy are four teenage girls who live in the United States of America. In a culture where it is normal for young girls of their age to get pregnant and abort as fast as you can say 'hot dogs', these girls decided to stand out. They not only began to speak against abortion before their peers, they decided to do something about it. They named themselves 'the saving arrows.' They identified an abortion clinic and would visit it each night to intercept abortions. How? They would initiate conversations with each girl as she approached the clinic. Sharing the love of Jesus, what he had done in their own lives and pleading with the girl not to abort the life growing in her but to consider giving the baby up for adoption. Even though they were not successful all the time, they were able to rescue many girls, after which they helped them locate crisis pregnancy groups to help them out. In the Bible we read about Daniel and his three friends who though in a strange land chose to be different. They were the best graduating students in the university of Babylon. God used them mightily to turn idol-worshiper King Nebuchadnezzar and his people to worship the only true God of heaven and earth. When your self-image is positive, it inspires you to be confident and purposeful in your lifestyle. Wherever you are, you become a change-agent and role-model. This is why it pays to be an eagle and make friends with fellow eagles!

What must you do to enlist in this elite corps who exert positive peer pressure?

You must change silly beliefs that make you yield to negative peer pressure.

Don't be Silly	*Be sensible*
1. I must dress, talk, and act like my peers or I won't be popular and I won't have friends.	I am unique, and as an eagle I don't have to be like others. I don't need to be popular; I only need to be what God wants me to be.
2. It is awful if others don't like me -my life would be terrible.	It is nice to be liked, but if others choose not to like me it is not the end of the world. God loves me no matter what.
3. I must please others and win approval all the time or else they will reject me and my life won't be fun.	I will try to do what is right, whether others approve or not. The only approval I can't do without is God's.
4. I should not make my faith in Christ a public thing. My peers will laugh at me and call me names.	I am an eagle. Even if my friends laugh at my faith, I will still talk about Christ. He is the saviour they need to get out of sin and from Satan's hook.

Whenever you find yourself under pressure to act or think a certain way, stop and say to yourself "Hey (your name) don't be silly, be sensible!" Once you learn to do this as a habit, you will begin to develop self-confidence. Soon your peers will realize they can't push you around and will begin to respect you. Before you know it, you will become a role model. That is how to exert **PPP** (Positive peer pressure).

That brings us to a tricky area where you must make up your mind to be sensible and not silly.

Lesbianism

Jane's story

"I never thought it could happen, but it did. It was an overnight church youth program. I was sleeping on a mat inside one of the church offices close to my friend, Cindy. Outgoing, and beautiful, at 17, Cindy was two years my senior. She was popular, intelligent and gifted. She could sing like a canary and play almost all the musical instruments. I often felt flattered that she liked me and showed it. I had always admired, respected and seen her as a role model. I had drifted off to sleep, when suddenly I jerked awake. What was that? Cindy was… kissing and caressing me! I was too shocked to know what to do. Her next words shocked me even further. 'Jenny, you know I love you. Please let's be lovers. Your body turns me on.' She whispered in a seductive voice. That was how it started. Cindy and I became lovers. She would shower me with gifts and love messages. I knew this was all wrong but I couldn't resist her. Each time I tried to let her see we were sinning, she assured me it was a wise way of escaping fornication. At the time I felt powerless, until I couldn't bear the guilt anymore. I phoned an aunty who was a very strong Christian and told her everything. That was the beginning of my deliverance from Cindy and lesbianism."

Thelma's story

"I had gone to spend the night with this family who were like guardians to me. It was a family I greatly admired. All were very active in church. Caro insisted that I share her bed. I didn't mind. She was my favourite. Although the youngest in the family, she was the most friendly and self-confident. Sometime in the middle of the night I felt hands on my body and pressure on my lips. I woke up with a start. It was Caro. I was shocked, but quickly realized what was happening. I

pushed her away as I sat up and said, "Never try this non-
sense with me again, ever!" After that we never talked about
it again; it was like it never happened. That's the only regret
I have. I guess I found it embarrassing. But I wish I had confronted her about it. Who knows how many innocent girls
she had succeeded in initiating into the dirty game?"

Thelma's and Jane's stories are a common teen experience
amongst girls. It happens often in girls' dormitories and at
home. The sad thing is that the Thelmas out there are a
minority. Sad too, not many are taking the bold step Jane took
after her initiation into what Thelma calls the dirty game. The
question is why do such things happen? Girls get into lesbianism for different reasons. The first reason is simply because
of the sinful nature of mankind. As human beings our hearts
and bodies constantly want to go against God's law. Another
reason is that a woman's body can be attractive, especially in
a sexual way. And that is why you must learn self-control and
discipline. That I feel like having sex with my cousin doesn't
mean I should yield to it. I simply talk to myself, *'Hey don't be
stupid, be sensible, this is wrong. Until I am married, sexual urge I will
not obey you.'* Once I do that repeatedly it sinks into my mind
and begins to control me, because all actions begin in the
mind. So you must get it into your mind that same- sex relationships are an abominable sin before God. God destroyed
the cities of Sodom and Gomorrah, because of their gay culture (Genesis 19, Romans 1:26-27). The Bible calls lesbian/
gay lifestyle unnatural relations.

*'Even their women exchanged natural relations for unnatural ones. In the
same way the men abandoned natural relations with women and were
inflamed with lust for one another'. (Romans 1:26-27)*

Other reasons girls get into lesbian relationships could be idle-
ness, pleasure, boredom, watching pornographic movies, peer
pressure, etc. Whatever the reason, any girl that falls into it
can be free. Whoever says otherwise is a wicked liar.

If you have already fallen into the trap, you can be set free. This is why Christ came, to set captives free. And the Bible says whosoever shall call on the name of the Lord shall be saved. Besides, you can talk to someone (but not a man). If you are sincere and truly want to stop the dirty and destructive game, you will find help. Never let anyone deceive you into accepting that you were created that way. God created male and female. God is kind; He has prepared someone close by to help you. Examples are your pastor's wife, female Sunday school teacher, an understanding female teacher, your mum, etc. If you choose to be an eagle in this matter, who knows, you might be opening the prison door to multitudes of girls who need to be set free too. And you will be proud of yourself for being an instrument that God can use and will reward you for that.

Set your boundaries

What do I mean by boundaries? Boundaries indicate limits or restrictions. When you know your limit in any situation, you can avoid making a mistake. In eating you must know your limits, if not, you bear the consequences. Freedom with no boundaries is irresponsibility, which leads to slavery or bondage. In any relationship, you must recognize and practice limits or restrictions. They help you keep friendships at a healthy level.

Learn to say no!

As an eagle one habit you must learn is to say 'no' when necessary, especially to your friends. If your parents say 'no' to a party – they do so because of their love for you. They know that all sorts of bad behaviours begin at parties. Many girls are introduced to sex, drugs, alcohol, lesbianism, etc. at parties. Remember Comfort who was drugged and raped at a party? But if your friends, who are ignorant and immature, like yourself try to oppose your parents' instruction and say:

"Don't be a kid, just sneak out or tell them that you are going for an all-night prayer meeting."

You must learn to simply say no and insist on no. They might say, *"Well, it means you are no longer our friend, you don't like us anymore."* If a person who claims to be your friend wants you to do what you know is wrong, just to prove you love them, realize that:

1. They want to step over your boundary – you don't need to prove anything to them.
2. They have no authority over you to make you obey them.
3. They want to trick you to do what they want.
4. They are liars if they claim to love you.

I know it is difficult to say no to your friend. She may interpret it as rejection. You may become scared that your friends will reject you too. Therefore, instead of saying no out-rightly you say, *'Ok, later"*, or *"I'll think about it'*. This is where your self-image plays a big role, because you are controlled by the way you see yourself. Lying shows you see yourself as a chicken. But you must determine to be an eagle, stand by what you believe. Don't be silly, be sensible. Look your friend in the eye and with a firm smile and a shake of your head from side to side say, *'No my dear, you are my friend but in this matter the answer is no and that's final, can we talk about something else?'*

If she insists or replies, *'I don't believe I'm your friend'*. Then you say, *'Well, the choice is yours, but my answer is still no'*.

Beware of girls who use gifts to manipulate others to do wrong. When you cheapen yourself to accept such expensive gifts as jewelleries, mobile phones, or pretty underwear from your peers, you weaken your conscience. If you accept a gift and you get asked to do what is wrong, quickly return it. Chickens can be bought with anything. But eagles can't be bought with anything, they won't compromise. That is, they won't go against their conscience or lower their standard for anything. Why? They know that all the gold or diamonds in the whole world are not enough to buy them, because they are made in God's image. Only the precious blood of Jesus Christ can do that. An eagle will smile and say, *'Thanks for your offer. I appreciate your generosity, but no thanks, I won't sell, I've already been bought!'* (by the precious blood of Jesus!)

For a while, you may seem not popular, but with time everyone will know they can't mess around with you. They will begin to respect and seek you out for advice when they have issues. You become a role-model.

Listen to your Conscience

God designed you with a conscience—an awareness of right and wrong.

It is a God-given inner voice, a built-in software, configured to guide you in life. It is the voice of your spirit. Anytime your Father (God) wants to speak to you, He downloads His mind into your spirit or the voice of your conscience (Prov. 20:27).

As an example, you may lie that you are going to pick a book from your friend's place, when the truth is that you planned to meet a guy at a hideout. This inner voice tells you it is wrong, but you may ignore or suppress it.

If you continually ignore this voice, a time will come when it becomes silent, so that even if you commit a terrible sin you would feel almost nothing. That means your software has become corrupted by the virus of sin! Your heart becomes as insensitive as stone.

You cannot hear God's voice in this state. However, if with determination, you train yourself to regularly listen to, and obey, the voice of your conscience, it will become very sensitive and sharp to readily receive from God; thus enabling you to make the right choices whether or not it is convenient. In that case you will not find it difficult to hear and obey God. This puts you in a position for greatness!

Discussion Questions

1. Who is a true friend? Read Proverbs 17:17 and Luke 1:39-56.

2. What is the difference between a healthy friendship and an unhealthy one?

3. What is peer pressure? Why do girls yield to it?

4. How does a girl's self-esteem affect her response to Negative Peer Pressure (NPP)?

5. How can a girl develop the boldness to exhibit Positive Peer Pressure (PPP)?

6. What are boundaries? What could happen to a girl who fails to set boundaries?

7. Read Jeremiah 35. What lessons can you learn from the Rechabites? How will you apply them to your life & when?

8. Mention and discuss some boundaries you have set in different areas of your life – e.g. "I will never visit or stay alone with a guy in a room or secluded place."

Chapter Five

She is wow!

Masingita Masunga-The Girl Who Chose To Love Herself

Masingita is a black South African. She suffered brain damage at birth. As she grew up it affected her overall skill in doing things. It also affected her speech, but it was obvious to all that she was a bright girl. Her parents refused to treat her like an invalid, which she gladly accepted. She giggles as she recalls, *'Some people thought I was being abused.'* About her disability she says, *'People don't understand me. They think because I talk funny, there's something wrong with my brain.'*

School was tough though; because it was difficult to understand her speech. But the girl's determination inspired her teachers to go the extra mile to help her. She even persuaded her schoolmates to ignore her disabilities and befriend her. High school was tougher still. She took an important exam and failed twice. She refused to give up and passed the third time.

Masingita always had a passion for beauty pageants and dreamed of being a beauty queen. After high school, she decided to start her own beauty pageant. The obstacles were great. But her total acceptance of her disability, and her ability to laugh at herself, drove her to succeed. In her first pageant, there were only 8 contestants with an audience of 20, but she made it.

Today she regularly holds beauty pageants for disabled girls from all over the country. In addition she is the Managing Director of a talent promotions company, as well as many other projects meant to empower the disabled. In 2004 she won a prize at the ShopRite checkers SABC2 women of the year award ceremony.

Self-acceptance

One wise, eagle decision you must make is to accept and appreciate yourself the way God made you. The truth is that none of us is perfect –each one has one flaw or the other. There is nothing you can do about your genes, which you inherited from your parents. They affect the shape of your nose, legs, eyes, height, colour, etc. If there is something you can do about a weak area, go ahead and do it. For example, if you have bad breath, brush your teeth after each meal and chew a minty gum; it will help to freshen your breath. Or if you have an offensive body odour, bath twice daily, use a body spray, or a sweet smelling talcum powder or rub lemon under your armpit. If you are overweight, cut down on junk food, eat more natural foods, fruits and vegetables. Exercise more and replace juices (artificial) with natural God-given water.

Self acceptance does not mean you deny what you don't like but you choose to say/think,

" 'I wish my legs were longer' or 'I would have preferred fuller breasts,' but since God chose to make me this way it means that's just the way he wants me to look for a purpose. His word says, 'I'm fearfully and wonderfully made', that must be true because God cannot lie. – I'm beautiful."

Self-acceptance produces peace and joy within you, plus it boosts your self-confidence. Like Masingita, you can even learn to laugh at yourself. When ignorant people laugh at you, it does not bother you because you have beaten them to it. When people meet you, they find themselves liking you without knowing why. It's because you have chosen to like yourself!

Don't let them fool you!

The TV and fashion magazines say: 'Thin is beautiful', 'Big breasts are hot', 'Figure 8 is it', 'short hair is the thing', 'shaved scalp is cool', etc. But you must not let anyone define fashion for you. These people who dictate the fashion trends are not reliable, rather they seem confused. There was a time pencil jeans were out, now they are in. Wigs were old-fashioned; now they are the trendy thing. Therefore you must let the beauty of God guide you in your choices. You can pick up ideas and inspiration here and there, but never let anyone distort your convictions about what is beautiful and attractive.

Don't let others think for you or set the pace, you are the pace setter. If you didn't know it, do so now! External beauty has never made people happy. Marilyn Munroe, a star Hollywood actress of the sixties, had the sexiest figure ever. Most women would have paid anything to look like that. But she committed suicide at age 36. External beauty does not bring fulfilment.

A beautiful wife of a president died because she was undergoing surgery to make herself look younger. Once on an Oprah Winfrey show, I saw the pathetic story of a young girl who refused to accept herself. As at that time she had undergone 12 plastic surgeries to make her look 'okay,' but she was still not satisfied —as I looked at her she resembled a sick Barbie doll. What a pity. You must learn to love your own skin.

Another thing you must not do is compare yourself with others. The Bible says it's foolish to compare. *'When …they compare themselves with themselves, they are not wise.'* (2 Corinthians 10:12) The Bible makes it clear that it is God by His wisdom and power who determined what part of the world we will come from and who our parents would be. Who our parents are and where and how we are brought up i.e. our background affects our looks and other things about us. God allows these differences because He has different desires, plans and purposes for different people. No wonder the Bible says it is foolishness to compare, because it is wasted effort and only brings misery and sadness. As I mentioned earlier, the wise thing to do is recognize our weak areas, do what we can to improve on them and leave the rest to God.

Rethinking Beauty

'The Lord does not look at the things man looks at. Man looks at the outward appearance, but the Lord looks at the heart' (1 Samuel 16:7). From this Bible verse we can see that true beauty is of the heart. Others may consider you beautiful, but if your heart is full of dirt, to God, you are ugly. Such dirt includes: greed, lying and deception, malice, pride, selfishness, gossip, sexual fantasies, fornication, pornography, etc. (Matthew 15: 19). The book of wisdom says a beautiful woman with no character is like a pig dressed up with jewels (Proverbs 11:22).

If a girl lacks the peace and love of God in her heart, no amount of make-up or designer fashion can help her. Until she repents and the blood of Jesus washes her heart, she is like a decorated doll- pretty but lifeless. Genuine beauty is much more than the redness of your lips or the glamour of your hairstyle.

A contented and cheerful heart is the secret of true beauty. If you invite the spirit of God He will come and dwell in you, and the fruit of the Holy Spirit is love, peace, joy, patience, kindness, etc. These qualities beautify you from within and enhance your outer beauty as well.

Discussion Questions

1. What is self-acceptance and how does it affect your life?

2. What have you not accepted about yourself, family, background etc.?

3. How can you accept yourself? Read Psalm 139.

4. Why should you not compare yourself with others?

5. How does lack of self-acceptance affect a girl?

6. What can make one a slave to fashion trends?

7. Why should a teen girl not be a slave to fashion trends?

8. What is true beauty? Read 1 Peter 3:3-4.

9. The concept of beauty is beyond your visual characteristics. Discuss.

Chapter Six

Help! I've fallen in Love!

There is nothing wrong or sinful in a girl being attracted to a guy, or the other way round! It is natural. God designed males and females to desire one another. This is known as the sex-drive. God intended to continue the human race this way- through a husband and wife and their children (Gen 1:26-28). Therefore when boys and girls reach adolescence (usually between 11 and 19), they suddenly begin to get attracted to persons of the opposite sex. Sexual behaviour (sex-drive) is controlled by the hypothalamus, an organ located in the brain. It stimulates the pituitary gland to release sex hormones. A hormone is a chemical messenger, which though secreted in one part of the body, goes on to tell other parts what to do. The secreted sex hormones in turn stimulate feelings or sensations towards the <u>opposite</u> sex. In girls the sex hormones are oestrogen and progesterone, and in boys testosterone. Due to ignorance most teens often confuse the feelings generated by these hormonal activities for love. We will soon see how this happens.

Since God created us male and female, these feelings of attraction (sex-drive) originated from Him. God is good (Psalm 106:1) and Holy (1 Pet. 1:15) therefore this attraction must be good and holy too. Problems arise however, because the sex-drive is not handled God's way.

How do sexual behaviours cause problems?

● Our immoral society

Our society is highly immoral. It's increasingly common to find young girls being sexually harassed and or abused at home by dads, cousins, uncles and other relatives. The molestation does not only stop there, it also continues in school, at the primary, secondary and tertiary levels. In addition, highly respected leaders and members of the society are known to have girls their own daughter's age as girlfriends and sex tools. We live in an age of sugar daddies (and mummies!). Sad but true, this wicked act even goes on in some churches as well. Cases abound where girls have been molested or impregnated by a church elder or a pastor.

● The media

Perhaps the biggest influence on teens comes from the world of entertainment through TV, movies, videos, and the internet. Others include magazines and books. And most of these have messages such as:

- Fun is okay at any cost

- Life is all about fun and pleasure

- Sex is the greatest fun, so get it at all costs

- Sex is ok, whenever and with whomever

- If it feels so good, it can't be wrong

- Sex is love

- If you feel like it, go for it

- The rich, the beautiful and famous are doing it, so it must be" ok etc.

Take for example, an advertisement showing a male celebrity and a beautiful young girl in a tight embrace. The celebrity has his condom ready for use in his pocket wherever he goes.

The advert is meant to influence young people towards 'safe sex.' Its message is:

'*This guy is rich, famous and the 'bomb', and his condom is always in his pocket, so be like him. To avoid AIDS keep your own condom ready and handy for action, you never know.*'

● Dysfunctional families

Dysfunctional families are families that do not function normally. Usually in such families:

- A dad is absent (physically or emotionally)

- Parents are separated or divorced

- Homes with frequent conflicts, violence, sexual or physical abuse

"Dad was never there for us, he lived his own life, in his own world. Mum was too busy with her job, friends and other men", Sheila an 18 year old girl shared with me. *"I wanted to be loved and protected, so I went with men my dad's age."*

Girls from such homes would tend to suffer from emotional and mental stress. These girls often experience anxiety, shame, low-self esteem and lack of confidence. Therefore they tend to be hungry for love and acceptance. Like Sheila, such girls are easy prey for any guy who comes along and says, "I love you", or "I'll take care of you."

● A deeper problem

There is another deeper root for the sexual problems we see today. Beneath the physical desire for sex and intimacy is a deeper spiritual hunger. Paschal, a French scientist says that within every human being is a God-shaped vacuum, which can only be filled by God. God created man to have a deep relationship with Him. The first commandment says we are to love God with all our heart, mind and strength. But that is not the case with a majority of us. We do not love God with such passion. We have diverted that passion to a wrong channel, so our hearts feel empty and hungry for God but we don't realize it. We also don't know how to satisfy that hunger or quench that thirst. So we turn to sex because it is readily available and pleasurable. But even after the act, the hunger and thirst remains, so we go for more sex and the cycle goes on.

It has nothing to do with poverty

Many say the key reason teenage girls indulge in sex or get pregnant, is poverty, but that is not true. There are many girls from rich homes who still give their bodies to men free of charge. Some girls even buy expensive gifts for guys they have sex with. No, physical poverty does not make people have sex. It is the poverty of heart or spirit that does that. A girl who is ignorant of God's purpose and plan for her life, or who knows, but chooses to reject God's plan will have sex for cash. But a girl who recognizes God's love and purpose will not, no matter her poverty. She will prefer to die than sell her body just for money. Marge told me, *'When I was in the university, I went through terrible financial struggles. Once, when my roommate went for classes, I went to pick food from her dust-bin to eat. I had so much pressure from men, but God helped me. I chose not to give my body to lecturers for money.'*

The word responsibility comes from two words: *response* and *ability.* You have the ability to choose your own response to any situation, no matter the external pressures. You have the power to choose to do right despite the actions of others. Therefore no one can excuse herself with, "I did not know" or "My friend or my dad/mum made me do it".

But I have fallen in love

So what do I do about these warm feelings I have? The butterflies fluttering in my stomach, the fuzzy-woozy, and nice feelings that rush all over me whenever I think of or see that cute guy? Do I just pretend these feelings are not there? Am I a bad girl for feeling this way? You are not a bad girl for feeling the way you do. These feelings are quite normal. What you need to know however, is that these warm nice feelings are not necessarily love. Besides even if they are for real, since you are not married, you must learn how to handle them correctly.

Falling in Love

What does it mean to 'be' or 'fall in love'? Is it the warm feelings of 'butterflies in the stomach'? For most adolescents, being in love is usually nothing but mere infatuation, or a crush.

<u>What is infatuation?</u> It's a state of temporarily being filled with intense, crazy, unreasonable love for a person. It can also be described as obsession or fascination with a person of the opposite sex.

<u>A crush</u> is a strong feeling of attraction, which does not usually last long. Girls usually mature emotionally faster than boys. So often, girls will fall in love with guys slightly older or much older than themselves e.g. a teacher, celebrity, etc. (We'll get to this later).

When a teen is in love, other relationships around her are affected as well. She may begin to isolate herself from the rest of the family, become secretive, or even tell lies e.g. say "I want to pick my text book from Mary" (lie!) Truth is, she has planned to meet Tom by the corner. She will leave chores undone, won't concentrate in class, spend hours day dreaming about him and reading phone messages from her 'Romeo', with whom she will ride away to a fantasy love-island where they will live happily ever after!

Usually two teens in love vow to love each other 'forever'. They love to spend hours saying sweet-nothings to each other. The young man declares, *"You are the most wonderful thing to happen to me!", "You are my angel,"* "*You are the only flower in my garden, and only star in my sky, " If loving you is wrong, then I don't want to be right! "* such words make the girl live on cloud nine!

Breakups and heartbreaks!!

Dan has not been calling and no text messages. He won't pick Lovina's calls and when he eventually did, he was not excited to hear her voice. He claims he is 'quite busy', and will 'call her soon' (lie!). To cut a painful story short – Dan has fallen out of love.

Breakups and heartbreaks are often inevitable in teen love. Tara is 16 and has just broken up with her 17-year-old boy-friend Brad. When she saw him curl his muscular arms around Tessy, she almost died with jealousy and pain. *"Oh my God, I feel terrible about myself. He promised that I would be the only love of his life. I feel so stupid and useless now,'* she said, as tears rolled down her cheeks. *'I wish I could die',* she sobbed. Why is Tara feeling so bad? She had had sex with Brad as proof of their 'everlast-ing' love for each other. She can't seem to understand what happened to the 'forever you alone love' vow he had made to her. Too late, she realizes Brad had only been playing games. Lizzy's story was different. She had fallen secretly in love with Mark, but kept it to herself. Mark has this brooding manner and deep baritone voice that just seems to melt the heart of most girls. Lizzy was however a self disciplined girl. She told herself to avoid Mark until she had gotten over her feelings. Two weeks later she saw him walking down a street hand in hand with a girl she knew. She silently thanked her God she did not make a fool of herself. She later told a friend "It's not worth it, it's nothing, it pays to be sensible."

You must understand teen love!

Often many teens talk about love with so much passion, with-out really knowing what they are talking about. Teen love is not recognized for what it truly is- an infatuation, a crush and mere fantasy. This should not be surprising, for this is a phase where teen emotions are still developing and not yet mature. As earlier mentioned, the build-up of hormones, especially during the ovulation (for girls) makes them feel sexually attracted to boys, but which they interpret as love. And for boys their sex hormones are most active from about age 17 years upwards. Therefore the choices and commitments teens make at this period are immature, childish and emotional (hormonal!). Emotions are not reliable; they are here one minute, the next they are gone with the wind! Or another kind of emotion may replace them.

Guys and Girls differ 'in love'

Everyone wants to be loved. It's a natural desire God put in each human being. It is especially so in a teenage girl. It is a powerful desire to be loved by a special guy she considers her own, who sees her and no other girl as special. But girls don't realize that most of the time when a guy says he "loves" a girl, he actually means she's beautiful and makes him experience feelings of sexual desire. It is a physical attraction stirred by sight (visual stimulation). So when the guy is talking of love, he means the girl's body, curves, pretty face and perhaps lovely voice all stir sexual feelings in him. And that is why a guy can tell three or four different pretty girls that he loves them. The truth is, he is physically and sexually attracted to all of them! But the only acceptable way he knows to say it is, 'I love you!'

Girls however are more emotional. They easily fall in love by what they hear and by touch. So a mere handshake or phrases such as, *'I love you'*, *'I can't resist you'*, *'I want you like I have never wanted any girl'*, etc. have the power to melt the heart of an inexperienced and immature teen girl. Her heart-beat increases and she feels this breathless mysterious feeling she has never felt before, tears of emotion might even come to her eyes! She therefore concludes, "I am in love!"

A girl at this time is not ready for sex but for love, romance and companionship. Her sexual maturity occurs much later than that of a guy. On the other hand the guy, though ready for sex, (his sex glands are most active at the late teen years), is not emotionally matured for love. So to get the sex he wants, he plays love. The girl being foolish gives in to sex to get the love she desires.

Sexual/physical attraction is not love

Mark says to Sheila, *"You are my angel; just the thought of you in my arms drives me crazy. Come on, show me that you love me or I'll die."* If Sheila were wise, she would say no and wait to see if he would actually die. But, Sheila replies, *"But Mark, we are still young, and we are both in school. Suppose I get pregnant?"* Mark will insist *"But it's ok, we love each other, and I want you like crazy. If you say no, it means you don't love me."* Sheila's heart rumbles with emotion and she thinks, "Oh no! I can't bear to lose Mark. We love each other and he is so romantic. If he didn't love me he won't want sex. And I really love him too." Sheila gives in. Just like many teens; she has been deceived into believing that sex equals love. Some months down the line Sheila gets pregnant and Mark makes his exit when Sheila refuses to abort. She wept as she narrated:

"He said he loved me and that I'll always be the only girl for him and the mother of his children. When I told him I was pregnant, He said, 'What do you want me to do? That's none of my business. You sort yourself out. We all have our lives to live.' I could not believe it, I was too shocked to speak."

Why do guys lose interest in girls after sex?

1. By nature, guys (men) are hunters. Once a girl has sex with a guy, the chase is over. He has made his catch. He begins to plan the next hunt.

2. The attraction cools off- you are attracted to the person that is hard to get.

3. She has shown him that she is just like other girls-cheap.

4. Girls usually expect that after sex the guy will love them more, but no way. They expect too much from him, almost as if he is a husband. So the guy gets choked by too much demand for attention and runs for his dear life!

Apart from sweet words, a guy may use a different approach to manipulate a girl into having sex. He may use rude and harsh words to intimidate a girl to give in to him. He might say, *'I saw prettier chicks like Milly, even Clara, but I chose you. Now you are acting like a primitive village girl, what a mistake.'*

This was Judy's experience. She was quite an eagle, but NPP (negative peer pressure, remember?) was harassing her through a guy named Thomas. His insults intimidated her, she even agreed with all his criticisms. By the time we talked she was close to giving in to him. I let her see that the guy was a chicken who wanted to lower her to his level. It was a difficult decision for her, but she ended the unhealthy relationship.

The story of Tamar in the Bible (2 Samuel13) is a classic example of the fact that sex is not love. Initially Amnon declared a passionate 'love' for Tamar. He said he was 'sick with love.' The guy was crazy about his beautiful step-sister. This was infatuation/obsession/fascination. That should warn any girl. If a guy becomes sick with love for you, run as fast as your legs can carry you. Sick love is sick, and it will make you sick in the end. If you were badly disfigured by an accident will he still be crazy or obsessed with you? After Amnon got what he truly wanted, sex from beautiful Tamar, the sick love flew out of the window. He hated her more than he had 'loved' her.

Are gifts and other favours a sign of love?

Stella was strongly convinced Jacob loved her because he showered her with plenty of cash, expensive gifts (shoes and clothes), stocked her locker with delicacies, etc. But after we talked and she refused to give him sex, he was furious and called her ungrateful and demanded back some of the expensive items. God helped her, she ended the sick friendship.

Because girls mature emotionally faster than guys, the tendency is that girls will usually find older guys more attractive. Another reason is that older guys usually have more money, are more experienced, more confident, and may have a car, can take a girl to fun places, expensive restaurants, buy expensive gifts, and know how to make her feel great and special! The girls however see this as love.

What is the truth here? That a guy buys you expensive gifts, and takes you to expensive places or gives you other favours, does not mean he loves you. He is simply using what he has (wealth) to buy what he wants, (sex). Once you don't service him with sex anymore, his real intentions are exposed. The guy might even be married, so he lies to you that his wife is a bore, old and ugly, but you drive him crazy. He may even convince you that he wants you as a second wife. This makes you feel great. The truth is, if he can do that to his wife, he can do that to you too. When he is tired of you, or he sees a girl hotter than you, he will throw you away like a pair of old slippers! I know there are some girls (chickens) who because of the goodies they get, don't mind being one of a chain of girlfriends or a second wife. Such girls have no vision or purpose in life. I pray any such girl reading this book will determine today to choose to turn her life over to Christ. He is waiting with open arms to receive you and give you a vision and purpose to live for.

Discussion Questions

1. It is wrong and sinful to fall in love. Give reasons for your answer.

2. What do you understand as the sex-drive?

3. What challenges do teens face in handling the sex-drive?

4. How does God expect us to handle our sex-drive?

5. What should a teen girl know about teen love?

6. How do boys and girls differ in falling in love?

7. Why would you say that gifts from a guy and sweet words may not be a sign of true love?

8. Why do guys often lose interest in a girl after sex?

Chapter Seven

Avoiding the Pitfalls of our Sexuality

In the previous chapter we established the fact that sex is not love. Making sex equal to love is one of the major lies that make teens engage in sex before marriage. But there are more lies. The devil, the author of lies, knows how destructive premarital sex can be, therefore he has cooked up many lies to deceive as many girls as he can.

More lies about sex

- If you don't taste sex now you won't have a good marriage, because you and your husband won't have experience.

- The boy may tell you he will get sick and die if you don't have sex with him, due to accumulated sperm.

- If you don't have sex, webs will grow in your private parts.

- If you don't have sex now you may not be able to get pregnant when you marry.

- It is old-fashioned to be a virgin- sex shows you are cool, civilized, fashionable sophisticated and ahead of your mates.

- Sex is ok, if you are old enough and you think you can handle it.

- If you feel like doing it and you don't, you are pretending.

- Once the desire comes it is impossible to say no.

- It will enlarge your breasts and buttocks giving you a 'wow' shape.

There are still many more lies, but the ones we have pointed out here should be enough to keep you from further ignorance and being deceived.

Reasons You Must Avoid Pre-marital Sex At All Cost

1. Emotional trauma

As mentioned earlier, the boy-girl relationship involves powerful emotions, and teens are not emotionally matured to handle these emotions. Usually when a teenage girl begins to indulge in premarital sex, the emotions involved consume her and she begins to act weird. She sneaks around, may be moody, lies, can't concentrate and often begins to perform badly academically in addition other areas of her life e.g. spiritual life, relationships are negatively affected, especially with parents or other authority figures.

This is why it is better to go by what the Bible says, 'There is a time for everything.' For example, jealousy can be a torture. Some teens become violent, when the one they "love" is seen with another or when the other person says it is over. It is worse when you have had sex because the emotional entanglement is such that you can't bear to be apart. After pleading again and again with 18-year-old Clara, she wouldn't leave the guy who she knew was cheating on her. She said to me, 'yes I know it's wrong to have sex with him, I know he may have other girls, and he is not likely to marry me, but I am unable to leave him.'

I saw on TV the true story of two teens, a boy and his girl-friend who committed suicide because their families were against their relationship and demanded they end it. Other emotions that torment teenagers include guilt, fear of preg-nancy, of being caught, of AIDS and other STDs, etc. Feelings of guilt make a teen lose confidence in herself and develop low self-esteem. Above all, guilt separates you from your God. You cannot pray. Even when you do, you don't expect answers.

Ruby, a younger friend, who was the leader of the teenage group in her church, once came to me and confessed that she had had sex with a guy. She could no longer stand the guilt and emotional ups and downs. As she recalled, prior to the act, she knew she had become lukewarm in her faith and had been drifting from the godly values that defined her life. Then she added, "I avoided anything and anyone that would bring me face to face with the truth about my shallow and casual attitude towards God. I particularly avoided my pastor and friends who were spiritually strong."

I tried to make Ruby see that running from confrontation with the truth was not in her best interest; that if she dared to face the truth, however bitter, she would experience the joy of forgiveness and a turnaround would follow (Isaiah 1:19). She also said that when her friend who was not a Christian asked her opinion about sleeping with her own boyfriend; she did not know how to help her. I let Ruby see that she was meant to be light to her peers; but she had failed on these occasions. But if she repented, her light would begin to shine again (Matthew 5:13-14). I also let her see that God still loved her so much and that whenever she found her-self drifting from the right path, she could always cry out to Him and He would come to her rescue. He may do so through authority figures like parents, aunts, uncles, older siblings, pastors, teachers, etc. Sometimes, they could be harsh and strict, and this could cause her to feel offended. Some may rebuke, encourage or advise her. Her response however would be determined by whether or not she had chosen to fulfil God's purpose for her life. If any girl must fulfil God's purpose for her life, she must be willing to listen to the authority figures God has placed over her and be ready to follow godly counsel.

"Stern discipline awaits him who leaves the path; he who hates correction will die" (Proverbs 15:10).

2. It's like digging your own grave!

When we visited Polly at the hospital it seemed like a nightmare. She looked like a cross between a scarecrow and a monster, with big red sores all over. As I looked in horror at the red gaping wounds, and bony frame I wondered, "Is any 'fun' worth this kind of agony?" I then recalled conversations we had had over her sexual relations with her boyfriend, who at the first sign of her illness (AIDS) took off.

STDs are on the increase among teens and many have no cure. HIV & AIDS has claimed millions of teens worldwide. Girls are the most affected. Left untreated, STDs have long-term health effects, especially for women.

Let's examine a few briefly.

Primary sexually transmitted diseases

Viral (Cannot be cured)

* Human Papillomavirus (HPV- the fastest spreading STD and the cause of virtually all cases of cervical cancer in women.)

* HIV/AIDS

- Cervical cancer- more women die from this than AIDS.

- Genital herpes- Manifests as open sores/blisters. It can be transmitted to the unborn child and can lead to severe birth defects.

Non-Viral (can be cured if properly diagnosed)

- Gonorrhoea- usually no symptoms (in women).

- Syphilis- infection leads to sores which can spread and cause fatal damage to the heart, nervous system and other body organs, e.g. brain, leading to mental illness (madness).

- Trichomoniasis- an infection of the urinary tract- may cause painful urination, can cause a woman to deliver a premature baby.

- Pelvic inflammatory disease can permanently damage the reproduction organs.

Knowing of these, do you now see why the Bible says anyone who sins sexually sins against her own body. ? *"All other sins a man commits are outside his body, but he who sins sexually sins against his own body."* (1Cor. 6:18)

3. Premarital sex entangles the soul

Sex is not just physical- organ-to-organ. It also involves your spirit because you are a spirit being. Your spirit or your heart is that inner invisible part of you which has the capacity to choose to respond to God or reject Him. The Bible says when a man and woman come together in the sexual act they become one flesh, meaning they become like one person. Sex bonds a man and woman together emotionally, physically and spiritually. What this means is that sex will introduce into your life the personality and spirit of the other person. Not only that, it robs you of part of your spirit as well. This is why long after sex, you and the person are apart yet you long for him even though you know it is wrong. Spiritually you have become one. If the guy has had sex with 7 other girls, their spirits are intertwined with his. By the time you have sex with him, you think you are having sex with one person, but in reality you are having sex with 8 people! Therefore girls who indulge in sex before marriage are usually weird in behaviour-senseless, reckless and stone-hearted. Sandra, 16, once knew God wanted her to write to inspire other girls, but that conviction flew out of the window after she began sleeping with her boyfriend. She would even beg for sex. If you don't repent, sex before marriage can rob you of your destiny and purpose.

'Do you not know that he who joins himself to a prostitute becomes one with her in body?' (1 Cor. 6:16).

4.   It will provoke the judgment of God

Your body is the temple of God who made you in His image. Sex corrupts your body, which is God's temple. *'...fornicators and adulterers God will judge'* (Hebrews 13:4b).
The Bible says the sexually immoral will never inherit the kingdom of God (1Corinthians 6:9).

5.   There are many risks related to it

a.   Before you can have sex with a man, you must be alone in a secluded place, naked and helpless. He would have aroused you to a point where you are senseless and totally at his mercy.

b.   He can drug you and do anything to you.

c.   He may stick anything into your vagina.

d.   He may have arranged with other rascals before you arrived and they could gang-rape you.

e.   He may kill you and use any part of you for a ritual.

6.   It is humiliating/shameful

Usually premarital sex occurs in dark corners, bushes, toilets, abandoned shacks, hideouts, hotels (cheap or expensive, far away from where you are known), in a classroom, etc. There is always the fear of being exposed. You must lie to continue to indulge in it. You must work hard to avoid pregnancy.

The experience is often disappointing

Read the confession of Paula who lost her virginity in a boy's school toilet.

"Why do people make so much noise about sex? It's no big deal. The pain was terrible and the blood scared me stiff. The stupid boy took my virginity at thirteen and dumped me. A pastor pretended (but I didn't know it then) that he was helping me by counselling. But he too sweet-talked me into sex again, then after it he pretended like I didn't exist and nothing had happened. God sent someone to rescue me the day I wanted to jump off a bridge into the rushing water below."

7. Teenage Pregnancy and motherhood

Often when a girl loses her virginity or becomes pregnant and has a baby, she seems to put on a tough 'I don't care attitude'. But this is really a cover-up for the shame and embarrassment she feels. No girl is ever proud of involvement in sex before marriage, ever! She becomes notorious as a sleep-around, the kind of girl parents warn their daughters to keep away from and most men may not want to marry.

If she gets pregnant and has a child, that child could become a constant reminder of her weakness of character and moral failure. What does she say when people ask about her husband or the father of her child, she either cooks a juicy tale or has to tell the embarrassing story again and again. It is however not the end of the road for any girl who gets caught in this trap. The forgiveness and restoration of God is readily available. There are compassionate counsellors who are skilled in providing care and counsel against the trauma of teen pregnancy as well as help those girls get their lives back on track. Such a girl with a strong determination and God's help can still become an eagle and achieve her dreams.

Jane's story

17-year-old Jane has been having sleepless nights for two weeks. When she slept she had nightmares. Why? Her period was late by five days. She didn't want to face the inevitable-pregnancy. She and Frank had been going out for 3 months. He was her second boyfriend. He asked for sex two weeks after they met. She pleaded with him to give her time. Eventually she gave in. She didn't want to break up again because of sex.

'Oh my God what will I do?' Out of panic she phoned Frank and blurted 'Frank I think am pregnant!'

'You are what?' He barked into the phone.

'Please, we need to talk'.

He never showed up until after a week. They ended up with arguments, accusations and counter-accusations. She wept in regret. Her greatest fear was her parents, especially her dad. Her friend Monica took her to a lab for a test. She lied she was 22 when the technician asked for her age. She almost fainted with tension as she waited for the results.

Teen pregnancy is quickly becoming fashionable, but that doesn't make it right. It is only so among chickens. Eagles soar on the wings of the fear of and grace of God. It is one of the most shameful and disgraceful things that can happen to a girl. That is why in the Bible God put a law that when a guy rapes a girl he must marry her. If she becomes pregnant as a result, then she is saved from the shame of single motherhood. Single motherhood from widowhood and divorce is a different kettle of fish. That is not what am talking about. That your mum, aunt or other celebrities you know are single mums does not make teen pregnancy and single motherhood right.

Children born out of wedlock undergo loads of emotional trauma, shame and ridicule. A guy in his twenties overheard a discussion that suggested that his mum's husband whom he always knew as his dad was not his real father. The pain he felt was unbearable. He confronted his mum and threatened to kill her if she didn't show him his real dad.

You must realize that the choice you make today doesn't just affect you but your kids and their kids and further generations. You have the power to set the stage for future generations to be blessed or cursed.

The Condom

You may call it the 'magic tool'. They say that if he wears a condom you cannot get pregnant. Though a condom is a type of contraceptive, that is, a device that prevents pregnancy, many teens do not read and so are unaware of the warning label on every condom package. If used properly, latex condoms will help to reduce the <u>risk of transmission of HIV/AIDS</u> and many other sexually transmitted diseases. It is also highly effective against pregnancy. Before using, read directions and warnings or caution. You need to know that the HIV virus which causes AIDS is only one tenth of a micron. A micron is one millionth of a meter. The smallest detectable defect in a condom is one micron.

What this means is that:

● The condom company does not claim to provide complete protection against either pregnancy or STDs. The truth is that there is still a risk factor associated with condom use. Many married women who use condoms as a means of family planning without other foolproof methods, are often surprised by pregnancy.

● Condoms can even break during sex.

● Condoms are not effective in preventing the spread of HIV, which is the most common STDs that has no cure.

● Some of the most common STDs are contracted by skin-to-skin contact on areas not covered by a condom.

● In spite of the increased use of condoms in the past 20 years, STDs have equally increased.

● While the use of condoms has increased among teens, STDs have also increased amongst them.

The condom is not the magic tool you think. Let no one deceive you. Even if a condom prevents pregnancy, it won't protect your heart from guilt, shame, or the judgment of God.

Contraceptives

Contraceptives are substances that prevent a woman from getting pregnant. There are different kinds of contraceptives.

Oral (pills) These contain artificial female sex hormones (oestrogen or a combination with progesterone made in form of pills). Users need regular medical check-up. Some of the side effects include weight loss or gain. It affects the menstrual cycle and causes hormonal imbalance.

Often they are manufactured and packaged in higher concentration than the natural hormones. So what happens is, if a girl takes these pills as directed, the pituitary gland is prevented from normal activity. Therefore the ovaries are not stimulated because the contraceptive (containing a high dose of artificial hormones) is high in the blood stream thus counteracting their activity. Hence they prevent ovulation, and subsequently conception.

Consequences

Due to the habitual use of artificial hormones, the ovaries are rendered dormant. In addition, the pituitary gland which at this adolescent stage is still developing is hindered from the normal course of development, especially the part involved in the control of reproductive organs. Therefore with continued use of these artificial hormones the pituitary becomes incapable of stimulating the ovaries to release the natural hormones at the right time. When this happens, by the time a girl is a woman and she is finally married and ready to have a baby, she may not be able to. This is known as *acquired primary sterility*, the cause of untold misery, regret and shame in the lives of many modern women.

Barrier method (Diaphragms and caps)

These are devices inserted into a woman's vagina which prevent sperm cells from reaching and fertilizing the eggs. They work best when used together with a chemical–spermicide which kills the sperms, because sperm can still escape through the barrier.

Contraceptive Injections

Contraceptive injections are an alternative to other hormonal contraceptives like the pill. They are made of a hormone similar to progesterone.

They are usually injected by a nurse or doctor into a muscle on the arm or buttock, and then gradually released into the blood stream.

Unlike the pill which needs to be taken daily, injections can last for up 12 weeks.

They work mainly by:

● Stopping the release of eggs from the ovary(ovulation).

- Forming a mucus plug which prevents the sperm from reaching the womb to fertilise an egg.
- Making the walls of the womb thin, therefore making it unlikely for a fertilized egg to be implanted there.

Side effects of Contraceptive Injections:

- When its use is continued, often leads to delayed return of fertility.
- Can negatively affect menstrual bleeding- cessation of menses or heavy bleeding.
- Risk of breast cancer.
- Irreversible bone loss.
- Can worsen diabetic, heart, stroke, liver, high Blood Pressure conditions.

Implants

These are soft tubes that slowly release synthetic progesterone. They are inserted under the skin of the upper arm under local anaesthesia. Some side effects include irregular bleeding, headache, and nausea. Removal can also be difficult.

Intra uterine device (IUD)

This is a small plastic and metal device placed in the womb. It does not stop conception but prevents a fertilized egg from being implanted in the womb. It is known as an abortifacient. Some side effects include heavy periods and the risk of infection. Therefore it is not recommended for women who do not have children yet.

Having briefly considered contraceptives and their side effects, can you see they were not made for teens? The health risk is too much. The only way to keep from pregnancy, is not to have sex. Make up your mind to be an eagle. The Bible records that nothing is impossible with God (Luke 1:37).

How to deal with 'smart lines' guys use to get a girl into sex.

Guy	*Girl*
If you love me you will show it by giving me sex.	If you love me you will wait till we are married.
Everyone is doing it.	I am not everyone.
A virgin at your age? You are old-fashioned.	No, I'm intelligent and focused.
I want to see and feel your sexy body.	You think I'm stupid?
You are hurting me.	You are insulting me.
You are driving me crazy.	Maybe you should see a psychiatrist.
You don't love me.	You don't respect me.
I want you to have my baby.	You are not my husband. I don't want bastards.

There are more, but if you truly determine to be an eagle, at each point you will know how to respond. Learn to look a guy in the eye and let him know you are not a mere 'chic.'

Abortion

Tito's story

Tito is a pretty but shy 16-year-old. She had a 19-year-old boyfriend in the university. One day she discovered she was pregnant. Afraid and confused he took her to a clinic for an abortion. Unfortunately her small intestine was perforated in the process. The doctor sensing she might die from chronic infection referred her to a teaching hospital for further treatment. Though the operation was successful, the infection had affected her womb. The doctor announced to the parents that she may not be able to get pregnant in future.

An abortion is the untimely termination of a pregnancy, by removing the embryo resulting in its death. The embryo is the baby still developing in the womb. Abortions can be spontaneous or induced. Often, many teens indulge in a type of abortion known as induced abortion. Induced abortion is forced or intentional abortion. Spontaneous/unplanned or natural abortion occurs when a pregnant woman has a miscarriage or when an abortion occurs as a result of an accident. Abortion can be therapeutic or elective. Therapeutic is when an abortion is recommended and carried out by a medical doctor to preserve the life of the mother. When an abortion is done for any other reason other than to save the life of the mother it is called an elective abortion.

Methods of abortion:

1. Medical
This is a kind of abortion where pharmaceutical drugs are used in combination with injections to kill and flush out the embryo. This method is effective in the first 3 months of pregnancy.

2. Surgical
This method uses various surgical instruments.

● Manual Vacuum Abortion (MVA)-a manual syringe or an electric pump is used to suck out the growing baby, placenta and other membranes from the womb.

● D&E (Dilation & Evacuation)-the cervix (opening of the womb) is opened and the growing baby is forcefully removed using a suction curette (a hollow tube with a sharp point at the tip).

3. Other methods (You need to note that the following methods are wrong and dangerous)

● A knitting pin or any sharp object can be inserted into the womb to pierce and kill the growing baby, which is later flushed out as blood. Some herbs can be used to poison the embryo, which is later flushed out through bleeding.

- A girl can choose to hit her abdomen with a heavy and large object to kill the baby.

- Drugs can also be swallowed to kill the growing baby.

  By the second trimester (4 months upwards) of pregnancy, other methods must be used. The method used is premature delivery caused by the combination of drugs and injections.

- After 16 weeks Intact Dilation and Extraction (IDX) is used. This involves a partial decompression of the foetus head before evacuation. Also known as partial birth abortion, it has been banned in the United States.

- From 20-23 weeks an injection can be given to stop the foetal heart, to ensure the baby is not born alive.

Is abortion murder?

Life begins at conception. A person can become pregnant one hour after sex. Fertilization often occurs 12-24 hrs after ovulation. The product of fertilization is called a zygote. It can be ascertained at this period whether the baby forming will be a boy or girl. If the zygote is made up of twins, by day nine after fertilization they will separate into two. By 11 to 12 weeks, the major body organs have started forming, e.g. heart, spinal cord, brain, etc. In the Bible we read the story of John the Baptist in the Gospel of Luke who was a foetus forming in the womb of his mother Elizabeth. When Mary the mother of Jesus visited and greeted her, Elizabeth observed that the baby in her womb 'heard the greeting' and 'leaped for joy'. Jeremiah was still in His mother's womb when God called him to be a prophet. What would have happened if Mary had aborted Jesus? What if the mothers of Nelson Mandela, Wangari Maathai, Barak Obama, Graca Marcel Mandela, Mother Teresa, or Mary Slessor had aborted them? God alone has the authority to give and take a life (1 Samuel 2:6, Psalm 139:13-16).

There is a better option to abortion:
Perhaps you find yourself in a situation where you don't want an abortion, but you are being pressured to have one. You don't have to. Talk to God your father. He says he will never cast away anyone that comes to Him. He will forgive you if you are truly sorry and are ready to start a new clean life. Let those who are pressuring you know you have decided to do God's will henceforth. The baby can be given up for adoption in a hospital or a motherless baby's home. If they refuse to listen, you can run away to seek help at a church or crisis pregnancy centre. I assure you, once you choose to please God He will back you up.

Dangers/risks of abortion

1. Incomplete abortion-some body parts or walls of the womb may remain inside the womb leading to infection-which can block the fallopian tubes causing infertility. It can also scar the entire womb, leading eventually to its removal. The infection can also spread through the blood causing death.

2. Kidney failure.

3. Damage to the bladder.

4. The uterus may be perforated leading to excessive bleeding and even death.

5. Problem with the anaesthesia can cause convulsions, heart problems and possible death.

6. The cervix can be sliced, cut, torn, etc.

7. Some of the herbs used are poisonous and can harm the mother herself.

8. Hitting the abdomen with a heavy object can damage internal organs.

Abortion is a horror story

<u>Ask Tammy</u>.
"It was horrible, I thought my insides were being ripped apart, I thought I would die, I wanted to die…."

<u>Rosa said</u>,
"I was later told by a neighbour who worked in 'the place' (abortion clinic) that I had aborted twins. For months I walked in a daze. Sometimes I heard the cries of babies even when no baby was around. I pretended it never happened just so I can go on with life. I even started drinking alcohol just to forget. Only God can help me now."

<u>Jolly</u>
"I was 15 when I found out my mum had tried to abort me by salt-poisoning. A solution of salt-saline was injected into my mum's womb. I was to die after gulping it, so my mum can deliver me dead 24 hours later. But I didn't die. Today I am alive but with a mental disability."

How does abortion affect girls who get involved?

Drug and alcohol abuse, shame, guilt, regret, anger, sleeplessness, low self esteem, depression and suicide attempts are some of the emotional effects. Every girl can make the choice that the horror stories of abortion will never be hers.

We have seen the ugly side of premarital sex and its consequences. Let's now see the true picture of sex as God intended.

Sex is God's idea

It might interest you to know that God and the Bible are not ashamed or the least embarrassed about sex. After all, sex was the original idea of a good and holy God. Apart from bearing children, God also created sex for pleasure between a husband and wife only. The Songs of Solomon is a love song between a bridegroom and his bride. It highlights the joys of sexual intimacy and passion between a bride and groom, not a man and his girlfriend or a girl and her sugar daddy or a girl and her boyfriend.

"So God created man in His own image… Male and female created He them and God blessed them and said unto them, be fruitful and multiply and replenish the earth.' (Genesis 1:26). *'Therefore shall a man leave his father and his mother and shall cleave unto his wife, and they shall be one flesh'* (Genesis 2:24).

Animals have sex-drives, but it is seasonal. The female allows the male to mate with her only when she's on heat. So once the female is on heat, she can mate with any male, anywhere, anytime! For animals, sex is just for procreation.

With human beings however, it is quite different. Sex is not only for procreation but also the most pleasurable, deepest, highest and most intimate expression of love between two married people. Unlike animals, humans don't have a seasonal but a potential sex-drive. This means that a husband and wife can live together without being controlled by sex.

You can't have sex all day but at the right time a married couple can stimulate each other for sex. It is only in marriage that the powerful sex-drive in humans can be met. But what happens is that often these passionate and powerful desires are aroused outside marriage, which leads to adultery, lesbianism, fornication, frustration etc. So for that reason, God gave clear guidelines to prevent frustration and fornication, and all the other negative, harmful consequences.

Two helpful insights on sex:

1. Sex is like a blazing log of wood

Sex is like a burning log of wood. In cold weather, in the fireplace, the burning log keeps the house warm and cosy. Family members love to gather round the fireplace to just hang out with one another.

But remove that burning log of wood and place it on a carpet in the centre of the room. Soon the house fills with smoke, people begin to choke and no one wants to remain in that house. The carpet may eventually catch fire and if not put out, it can burn down the whole house. Sex is good, but if taken out of its protective boundary of marriage, it can become a raging fire that consumes and destroys. Sex therefore though refreshing, could be dangerous outside God's guidelines.

2. Sex is like a bouquet of flowers

Sex is like a bouquet of white roses. If placed in a vase, it is beautiful and can transform even a small hut into a lovely place. Remove the bouquet and throw it on the floor, or a chair, someone may sit on them; the tender petals may be trampled upon, crushed and killed. Sex, like the flower, should be preserved in the flower vase; which is marriage or it could be destroyed. Sex, is both beautiful and delicate, so it needs to be protected. God, the author of sex is a wise and loving God. Knowing that we are weak humans, He gave laws to protect sex and so protect us from the harmful effects that result when sex is not handled right.

How God protects sex to protect you

● Through customs/culture
In almost every culture and religion, sex before marriage is a taboo. Most cultures demand marriage rites before a man can sleep with his wife. Why? God put the knowledge of right and wrong in every human heart. (Romans 1:19).

● In the Old Testament, the Bible considers sex before marriage as a capital sin, punishable by death! The Bible also forbids any sexual contact with children, step-children, parents, step-parents, brothers, sisters, step-siblings, aunts, uncles, in-laws or with the same sex-lesbianism/homosexuality (Leviticus 18. 7-18; Exodus 20:34).

- The Bible makes it clear that a sexual fantasy is actually like the sex act itself. God demands purity of heart as a protection. Pornography or any activity that stimulates the mind with sex is also forbidden. (Matthew 15, Matthew 5: 27-28, Proverb 4:23).

- Sex with anyone who is not your spouse is forbidden.

  When Potiphar's wife tried to seduce Joseph, he ran as fast as his legs could carry him! (2 Timothy 2:20, 1 Corinthians 6:18).

- If you claim to be born-again, it means Christ is living in you. If you commit fornication, you are making him partake of the sinful act. (1 Corinthians 6:15-16).

- In Jewish culture if a guy rapes a girl, he must marry her because he has dishonoured her and no one would want to marry her. Deuteronomy 22:28-29).

As I end this chapter let us examine the lives of two girls-Lori and Pamela, one an eagle the other a chicken.

Lori (an eagle)	*Pamela (a chicken)*
1. Is happy, feels good about herself.	1. Often moody, tense, lacks confidence.
2. Has no worries, determined to be a virgin till marriage.	2. Worried about STDs, pregnancy, abortion, being caught.
3. Relates with eagle guys who know her stand and so don't demand sex.	3. Has sex with her boyfriend, worries he doesn't love but is using her.
4. Close to her parents, especially mom.	4. Lies to her parents, sneaks around, has secrets.
5. Dreams about a career as a medical doctor and a loving marriage to a godly guy.	5. Worries that everything about her future is uncertain.

Discussion Questions

1. What are the common lies about sex?

2. Why do teen girls often engage in premarital sex?

3. Mention reasons why a girl should avoid sex before marriage?

4. What are contraceptives and how beneficial are they to teen girls?

5. How can a girl avoid teen pregnancy?

6. How can teen pregnancy affect a girl's future?

7. What are the dangers of abortion?

8. What should a girl do if she is being pressured into abortion or sex before marriage?

9. Read Proverbs 5, 6:20-35 and 7. Identify the dangers of sex outside marriage highlighted in these three passages.

Chapter Eight

Understanding & Overcoming Sexual Abuse/Harassment

Before we talk about sexual abuse, let's begin with sexual harassment, which often progresses to abuse. Sexual harassment is when someone talks about your body in a sexual way, makes sexual comments, continuously pesters you for a date or touches you in a sexual manner, which offends or annoys you. The harasser is often in a position of power or is bigger/stronger than the person harassed. So they will often use intimidation, bullying and force. The person may promise you money, expensive gifts, marriage, scholarships, high grades, etc. in exchange for sex.

An abuse is when something is used in a wrong or harmful way. Sexual abuse is when anyone touches you in a sexual way, like fondling your breast or buttocks, exposing you to pornography, exposing their genitals to you, kissing, inserting anything into your vagina or anus or any other kind of caressing that stimulates you sexually without your permission. If the molestation lasts for only a short time or is infrequent it is described as an assault- an example is rape. Sexual abuse is wrong, no matter who does it to you. Like we earlier mentioned, your body is a restricted zone, nobody has the authority to talk to you or touch you in a sexual way, except your own husband.

Signs of sexual abuse of harassment

Remember that you are made in the image of God, which means that part of God's personality lives in you. So learn to trust your instincts. When someone tries to do something wrong to you, your conscience will alert you. Don't ignore it. Pay attention and respond with courage. Here are examples of off-colour phrases that are indications of sexual abuse.

A respected individual, perhaps an uncle, a cousin, your friend's dad, a teacher, etc., begins to make comments that make you uncomfortable, such as:

"You have a sexy body, take this money and buy a nice outfit."

"Come and sit on my laps."

"What is the size of your bra?"

"Can we meet at (any secret place) tonight? Make sure you tell no one."

"These are the questions for tomorrow's exam—don't you tell no one?"

"Bolt the door and come give me a kiss".

They may pester you with calls or send you indecent multimedia/text messages/pictures etc.

How do you respond to harassment or abuse?

<u>Eagle response</u>- Your response will depend on who you think you are and how you see yourself, that is, your self-image. Remember, you are controlled by the way you see yourself. If you recognize that God the Creator of the universe is your dad and that He created you for a unique purpose and has a specific plan for your life, you will have a positive self-image.

Therefore your response will be like that of an eagle- bold and courageous.

<u>Chicken response</u>- If you think of yourself as worthless, ugly, hopeless, it means your self-image is poor . Your response will be like that of a chicken-timid and fearful. You may likely cry or allow the person to bully you into doing what your conscience tells you is wrong.

It is wise to arrest harassment before it progresses to abuse. Remember the signs of harassment we mentioned earlier. You must summon up courage and pray for boldness and wisdom. Look the culprit in the eye and tell the person:

'I won't enter your house or bedroom when no one else is there.'

'Please, I don't like being hugged that way.'

'Don't say such words, they are bad.'

'Please don't pat me on my bum/touch my breast again. It is wrong/it is not decent/ I don't like it and God doesn't.'

'Don't send me such messages or I will tell so and so.' (Let it be somebody you know they fear and respect).

'Thanks for your offer but I won't accept it. I prefer to study hard for good grades. Cheating is wrong and a sin.'

If the person tries to make it seem okay, insist that you won't give in to their demand. Respond with confidence:

'It is not right because I am not your wife.'

'My body belongs to God.'

'This is a sin.'

If your heart is pounding, calm down, take a deep breath, pray 'Lord help me', 'protect me', 'make me bold', 'send help to me.'

Stand up if you are sitting (It boosts your confidence).

Talk loudly, don't whisper or stammer (don't shout yet).

Look the person in the eye.

Don't look down at your feet or pretend to draw on the floor with your toes (It's a sign of timidity and the other person will take advantage of that).

Don't twist or rub your hands together, it shows you are nervous and confused.

Express your thoughts aloud e.g.

"-I can't believe this daddy/uncle, pastor/Mr. John

-I have always respected you,

- I thought you feared God, why are you doing this?

- Would you like mum, aunt, pastor, granny, etc, to know what you are trying to do?"

If the advances persist:

- Refuse to give in- become angry and stubborn.

- Keep praying about it and talk to another person (but not a peer).

- Talk to a parent, a godly and trusted female pastor, teacher, friend. Let it be somebody mature, wise and who can handle it. I plead with you not to be ashamed or afraid of speaking out. You have not done anything shameful. Besides, you will be helping the person molesting you. What they are doing shows they have a problem. Even if the person is related to you, please don't hide this evil from wise and godly persons around you.

- Get as far away as you can from this person-scream if needbe.

- Seek help immediately- run away if need be, your life and future is in danger!

- Call/shout the name of JESUS. Shout "In Jesus name leave me alone. I belong to JESUS, God is my father, and you have no right to touch me."

- Remember what we said in chapter 1 about Mordecai?" God is so kind; that no matter your situation, there will be a trustworthy and wise adult you can talk to or run to for help.

What can attract sexual abuse?

Sometimes a mother can be the one who introduces her daughter to abuse. Lara's mom is a single mother whose boyfriends come to spend the night often. One of them would often visit when he knew her mom wouldn't be in. He would give her gifts and engage her in endless and meaningless talk Finally one day he attempted to kiss her by force. That experience made her bitter and she became a wayward girl, selling her body to any man who is ready to pay. Some moms will send their daughters on errands to their boyfriends or to a wealthy man who helps the family financially, thereby creating opportunity for these irresponsible adults to take advantage of them. Sometimes a girl can invite abuse by being too close to a teacher or any other man for favours. If you are like that, stop it now for your own good. If you continue you are selling your soul to the man and the devil. No matter your need, if you cry out to God He will meet it.

Not easy, but possible

Sexual harassment or abuse is a very difficult experience for any teen girl. The eagle responses suggested above are not easy, but with God's help you can do it. Sexual abuse is often carried out by an adult who though appears normal, actually has a problem. If you have already participated in it, don't think it's your fault or that you deserve what is happening to you. Even if you caused, you can quickly repent. You may even have enjoyed it, so you feel guilty about that. But the truth is that the person took advantage of your ignorance and natural sexual feelings. The person may want to convince you that it is love. This is a big lie. He may shower you with expensive gifts to keep you from exposing him. The person may be paying your fees, or helping your family financially, so you feel you owe them something. Giving your body to them is not the way to show gratitude, you can run errands or do other services. He may give you high grades, but he wants to destroy your future not help you. If you are in high school now, he won't be there when you need to write a national or university exam. He won't be there when you go for a job interview.

He may threaten you that if you refuse or expose him/her, you will fail the exam, he will stop helping your family, you will die or something terrible will happen to you and those you love. A high-school teacher abused his students for years. He threatened each one that something terrible would happen if they told anyone. None did, but eventually a girl could hold it no longer. She poured out the whole ugly story to her mum. The teacher was arrested. Refuse to be intimidated with threats which are a means to cover up his fears. He knows he is committing a terrible crime punishable by law, so he/she is afraid. If you let him/her intimidate you with fear, you will become his/her slave forever, and you will never know the life of peace and joy that God planned for you. Whatever the case, you must expose him/her; God will protect and take care of you. When Esther, Daniel, Shadrach, Meshach and Abednego took risky steps because they wanted to please God, He intervened on their behalf (Dan. 3:13-26, 6:10-19, Esther 4:16,). He will do the same for you.

The Lord is the stronghold of my life-of whom shall I be afraid? When evil men advance against me to devour my flesh, when my enemies and my foes attack me they will stumble and fall. (Psalm 27:1-2)

Also, refuse to let your mom or any relative pressure or manipulate you into a situation of abuse. If they insist, you can run away to a church, a godly woman or pastor for help. Also if your mom is the one exposing you to or arranging the abuse, this is one situation you must disobey. Refuse to be manipulated into evil. The Bible says it is better to obey God than men, and we are told to obey our parents only in the Lord (Acts 4:19, Eph. 6:1-2).

This is the true story of a young woman who was sexually molested as a child.

The damage has already been done. Whether I will be able to deal with it, I don't know. I know from painful personal experience that the only way it (sexual abuse) will stop, is if you talk about it, because if you remain silent, that demented freak will just carry on and ruin another innocent life. I always felt guilty after the act ended. I guess that's why I never told anyone. It is so disheartening that we are so many and we keep quiet. I know there are many more like me suffering in silence, telling themselves that it happened a long time ago, that it shouldn't matter, that it's water under the bridge. How many mothers, fathers, brothers and sisters veil these wicked and appalling acts committed against children because they feel exposure would bring shame to their families? Don't they realize what their kids go through and will still go through? Don't they know that they are destroying their children's lives when they don't speak up? This emotional baggage is almost impossible to shed when one is grown up. It doesn't ever go away until you deal with it. Never allow yourself to be overwhelmed by shame or embarrassment. It is your abuser/harasser, not you, who is guilty, therefore he should be ashamed and embarrassed. Again, never withdraw, keep quiet or distant from other people who can help you. There is a being known as the devil – he is a liar, deceiver and destroyer (John10:10, John 8:44). So he can make you feel and think there is no one you can trust and you feel bad, lonely, lost and hopeless. By the time the devil backs you into a corner, he strikes with the suggestion of suicide. Refuse to listen to him.

Sylvia, an 18-year-old was so overwhelmed by her situation. She deliberately walked into a busy road hoping to be killed by a car. But she soon came to her senses. She said, "I prayed that God would lead me to someone to talk to." And God did. Today she is a happy teen, with plans to help others by writing about her experiences. You too can receive that help, if you truly want it. Only, you must be determined and desperate enough to look for it. God will send help to you wherever you are.

'Where does my help come from? My help comes from the Lord... (Psalm121:2).

Joyce Meyer, a popular American speaker and author, often shares about her own dad who sexually abused her from childhood until she became a teenager and ran away from home. If she had committed suicide she won't be the accomplished author, preacher and blessing she is to millions today. God not only healed Joyce Meyer, He gave her grace to forgive her dad, and mum (who knew about it, but did nothing). Through God's intervention, Joyce Meyer led her dad to Christ and one day baptized him! What He did for Joyce Meyer and Sylvia He can do for you too.

Effects of sexual harassment/abuse:

1.   Guilt, self-blame and shame.

2.   Nightmares, sleeplessness and low self esteem.

3.   Fears, anger, anxiety and depression.

4.   Headache, weight loss or weight gain,

5.   Loss of concentration, thoughts of suicide, mental illness.

Rape

Rape happens when a girl is overpowered by a man and forced into sexual intercourse without her consent. This also includes sticking an object into her anus or vagina. Research shows that teenage girls between sixteen and nineteen years are four times more likely to be raped than any other age group. Rape, though an unfortunate social vice, has become quite common.

Why do men rape girls?

There are no easy answers. But some of the causes of rape are:

—Most men who indulge in rape are also involved in drugs alcohol, violence, etc.

—Some of them have emotional and psychological problems, e.g. anxiety, disappointment with life, shame, etc.

—On the spiritual side, the devil is on a mission of destruction, and rape is one of his weapons (John 10:10, 1 Peter 5:8).

Whatever the case, you can minimize your risk of being raped by doing the following.

1.   Never agree to be alone with a man in a house, room, car, toilet or any other secluded place.

2.   Refuse to meet a man/boy in a secret hideout or dark area.

3.   Don't visit a boy alone.

4.   As a teen, don't have a secret relationship with any boy or man. Your parents or guardian must know anyone, especially if of the opposite sex, that you are in a relationship with.

5.   Usually our family members should be trusted. But some may be wolves in sheep clothing. If you ask the Holy Spirit

to be your guide, He can alert you to family members you should not trust. Also, do not ignore any warning signs and your intuition about a family member who may be a potential abuser.

6.   Beware of that cousin or uncle who is an alcoholic, who uses dirty language, cracks dirty jokes, likes to touch you often and gives you that look that makes you uncomfortable.

What to do if you are raped

● Call or quickly go to a friend, pastor, or woman you trust and feel safe with.

● Don't shower or change your clothes.

● Go to a nearby hospital-the better if it is a women's hospital.

● Seek spiritual help/healing from a godly woman you trust.

● You must seek help, even if it happened many years ago.

● Don't let shame stop you. If you don't seek help, you may endanger your health. You may have contracted a life-threatening disease.

● Refuse to panic even when people disbelieve you or react negatively towards you.

● Trust God to lead you to kind and godly people who will believe and stand by you.

● This is the time to call on God and have faith that He will intervene.

A lot of times many girls are intimidated because they are ignorant of their rights as girls. I pray the few I mention here will cure you of some of that ignorance.

Some key rights of the girl-child

● A healthy and safe environment.

● Freedom from cultural practices, customs, and traditions harmful to the child, including female genital mutilation, etc.

● Protection from all mental and physical abuse.

● Protection from all economic and sexual exploitation, prostitution, trafficking, etc.

● Freedom to express an opinion about plans or decisions affecting the child's life.

You must receive help from God to speak up and resist any one who may want to abuse any of these rights. God your father will fight for you.

Discussion Questions

1. What is sexual harassment or abuse? (SH/SA)

2. How would you know that you are being sexually harassed or abused?

3. What could provoke SH/SA and how can you avoid it?

4. How should an eagle respond to SH/SA?

5. If you or a girl you know has been raped, what should you or the girl do?

6. Why should you not keep quiet about sexual abuse or rape?

7. What are the likely effects of SA/SH?

8. What are some of your rights as a girl?

9. Read Leviticus 18.

Chapter Nine

The Desire of every Girl

In previous chapters we made it clear that sex, gifts, sweet words and other attractions are not love. If so, we have a big question to answer.

What then is love?

Some young people's definition of love

→ Love is a strong feeling

→ Love is emotional measles

→ Is a feeling you can't explain

→ It is affection for some one

→ Butterflies in the stomach.

Some false ideas others have about love:

● Love is a mysterious visitation which comes out of nowhere and grabs you; it is recognized by intuition, once it is there, no one needs to tell you because you will know it.

● Love is so important that you must give up everything for it. A man is justified for leaving his wife for it, a woman can abandon her husband and children for it and a king his throne for it.

● Love may disappear as suddenly as it comes. There is nothing you can do about it; it cannot be controlled by humans.

Before we begin to define and discuss what true love is, we must first recognize that there are basically three kinds of love.

1. **Agape love:** The most important and greatest kind of love is known as agape love. 'Agape' is a Greek word used to describe a special type of love. There is no English word for this kind of love. Agape love is the highest kind of love. It is that love which is willing to give and sacrifice for the highest good of another person. There are two main attributes of agape love –first, it is totally unselfish, and it seeks what is best for the other person. Secondly, it is committed – no matter what happens, it keeps on loving. As a girl you should develop agape love for everyone. As you relate with guys and they profess love, ask yourself 'is this agape'? The only kind of love that brings lasting joy and fulfilment in marriage is agape love. And only eagle guys have the ability to express agape love. Watch out!

2. **Friendship love:** It is the warm affection or likeness one can have for a dear friend, sibling, etc. usually these are people whose company we enjoy, like to talk to and generally feel free with. A girl should have such friends both as guys or girls.

3. **Sexual love:** This is the most intimate kind of love that should exist only between a husband and wife. This love exists at the top of our pyramid, and shows that this kind of love is exclusive, or reserved. It is never general.

Now let us go on to discuss what true love is.

Love *is* more than just a feeling. Love is the willingness to put the well being of another at the expense of self. It means being able to sacrifice what I want for the sake of another. Love seeks to give rather than demand. The greatest expression of love is that which God made by giving His only begotten son to die for mankind. '*… in this the love of God was made manifest among us , that God sent His only son into the world , that we might live through Him.*' (1 John 4:9)

Love is action; it is beyond words or feelings. 1 Corinthians 13 best expresses what true love is.

Love *never gives up.*

Love *cares more for others than for self.*

Love *doesn't strut.*

Love *doesn't have a swelled head.*

Love *does not force itself on others.*

Love *isn't always "me first".*

Love *doesn't fly off the handle.*

Love *takes pleasure in the flowering of truth.*

Love *doesn't keep a score of the sins of others.*

Love *doesn't revel while others grovel.*

Love *puts up with anything.*

Love *trusts God always.*

Love *always looks for the best.*

Love *never looks back.*

Love *keeps going to the end.* (MSG)

Two Love Stories

Tim and Tracy met at her cousin's birthday party. Tim sang a solo and played the guitar. Tracy was instantly attracted to this cute guy and after they were introduced they hit it off immediately.

Her admiration for him grew even stronger when she discovered that Tim was not only funny, but intelligent (she called him a mobile Internet!) and responsible. When she wore a blouse that revealed too much he nicely asked her to wear something more decent. He challenged her in her weak subjects, even going to her house to coach her. With time her physics and math's improved. Her appearance too, because Tim always insisted that she dress like the queen she is, not like 'them.' But one day they found themselves alone. Before they knew what was happening, they were kissing and losing control. Tim came to his senses first and gently pushed her away. 'Tracy, I'm so sorry, forgive me for I can't do this to you. We must never let this happen again. If this is meant to be, I prefer we do it at the right time.'

Often a guy will say to a girl I 'love you', but the truth is, he 'lusts her.' what he actually has is a mere strong sexual desire for her.

Jacob and Rachel

The Bible records the wonderful love story of Jacob and Rachel. Jacob loved Rachel so much he was willing to wait and work for fourteen years in order to marry her. You think he grumbled through those years? No way! Those years seemed like weeks because of the love he had for her (Genesis 29:16-30).

Let's distinguish between true love and lust.

True Love	*Lust*
You can be yourself	You pretend in order to be accepted
There is concern for the other person's welfare	Concern is for what I can get
Allows you to follow your own goals	Compels you to follow others' goals

Persons involved can be apart	They must be together
There's honesty about issues	Hides the truth and hides from the truth
Gives and is satisfied	Takes and is insatiable
Attracted to the total person	Attracted mostly to the physical
Grows over time, as you know him/her better	Usually catches quickly like fire!-without a real knowledge of the other
It brings out the best in you, a maturity and desire to plan for the future	It brings out the worst –you become childish, only inter-ested in now

Lakita Garth is a singer and rap artist– she was Miss Black California. Her grandfather and grandmother were married for almost 70 years before her grandmother died. He contin-ues to visit his wife's grave side every day, 'to be with my best friend', he says. Lakita said:

"I made a decision that day that I would rather be with one person for 70 years than be with 70 people in 70 years. I made a decision to save my heart and my body for the man I will one day marry and love for the rest of my life."

You may be reading this and feel you are truly in love and that the relationship is for real. Teen love may sometimes actually develop into mature love, leading to marriage. But how do you determine whether what you feel is true love or not?

Test of true love

1. **The admiration test** – apart from having nice feelings toward each other, there must be other reasons why you are attracted to each other, e.g. he is very responsible,

polite, loves God, focused, respects my beliefs, intelligent, has dreams similar to mine, etc.

2. **The habit test** – do I want to spend my entire life with him if his habits never change? E.g. smoking, hot-temper, taking alcohol, interested in pornography, lying, etc.

3. **The sacrifice test** – are you both willing to give up something each enjoys for the other? Is he willing to wait till marriage before sex?

4. **Talk freely test** – can we be sincere and talk freely with each other about any issue?

5. **Knowing each other test** – have we taken time to know each other's past and present, hopes , dreams , family, values, spiritual beliefs, goals and aspirations?.

6. **The love for Christ test** – are we both influencing each other to know Christ more? Do we enjoy serving Christ together or is it just one of us that is really interested?

7. **The distance test** – if it is infatuation, separation (change of location or a long travel) will kill the relationship. But if it is real love your hearts grow fonder for each other.

8. **How do others see your relationship?** What family and friends who love you both observe and say is extremely important.

9. **Effect on personality test** – infatuation disorganizes and brings out the worst in you-you become childish and senseless. True love does the opposite, it excites you also, but it brings out the best qualities in you, you become mature.

10. **The quarrel test** – in infatuation you quarrel too often over trivia, but soon make up with kissing and even sex. But with time, the quarrels become more severe and irresolvable. In true love, you quarrel too, but they become less frequent and severe as the two of you get to know each other better.

I pray that you will be sincere as you use these tests to evaluate your relationship whether it is true love or infatuation.

It will be wise to sit with this guy at this stage and discuss your relationship openly and honestly. If you are not able to do this (test 4), then it is already a clue that it may not be true love. If you have already had sex with this person, the sexual attraction will be so strong that you may confuse it with love. But if you base love on sex, that relationship is doomed for failure, because sooner or later the guy gets bored and looks for other sweeter game. But it's never too late to start on a new path. Time is one of your best friends; give yourself and the guy time. Never be in a hurry on the matter of marriage. One big favour you will do yourself at this stage is to seek godly counsel and prayers from a matured godly woman, pastor, etc. Though very painful, a broken courtship or engagement is far better than a broken marriage.

Discussion Questions

1. What is love?

2. What are some false ideas people have about love?

3. Mention and discuss the three types of love.

4. What kind of love is needed for a lasting and happy marriage?

5. How can you tell the difference between true and false love?

6. What are some of the tests of true love?

7. When it comes to the issue of marriage, what must you never do?

8. Read 1 John 3:16-18 and Matthew 1:18-19.

Chapter Ten

The Limits of Guy-Girl Friendship

Every girl has the opportunity to interact with boys in different situations e.g. school, church, camp, neighbourhood, etc. And sooner or later girls and guys begin talking of going out together or dating.

What is dating?

To date means to go out with a guy at a particular time that both of you agree on. A date could be single, double or group.

→ Single- you and a guy go out alone.

→ Double- 2 guys and 2 girls go out together.

→ Group- several boys and girls go out as a group.

Dating is not necessarily a sin but can lead to sin if care is not taken.

When is a girl old enough to date?

● When you recognize the advantages and disadvantages of dating.

● When you realize that as an eagle you must date only eagle guys.

- When you have personally recognized a Biblical standard that will guide you.

- When you have made up your mind never to lower that standard.

There are a few advantages of dating, for example:

→ It can help you develop socially, as you mature and learn to relate with guys and girls in different situations.

→ It can help you learn to be at ease before guys.

→ And it can help in choosing a life partner.

The truth is that you can equally achieve these without dating.

What are the disadvantages of dating?

1. It promotes flirting, show-off, and jealousy as you change dates, leading to broken hearts.

2. It often leads to unnecessary closeness and eventually sexual intimacy.

3. Can lead to an artificial relationship, where the girl and guy try hard to impress each other.

4. It can leave a girl wounded and battered like a banana that has been handled by 100 people.

Why do teens date? Here are some teen responses:

- Recreation-my age-mates are dating, it's also to have a good time and to socialize.

- Companionship-good to have someone I enjoy spending time with.

- Intimacy-I need someone I can trust to share my thoughts.

- Status-dating makes you look special before your peers.

- Sexual activity-from kissing to more 'serious stuff.'

- Experience-to discover how to act with the opposite sex.

- Marriage-to find a future partner.

Teen years- a time for foundation laying

A three-storey building collapsed in a busy part of a big city. Nine people including three children died with several injured. The cause of the tragedy was a faulty foundation. Don't let that happen to you.

- This is the time to build a strong foundation for your future. Let yourself develop and mature in all areas of your life.

- It's also a time to concentrate on becoming the best that you can be academically.

- Discover and develop your gifts and talents as well as learn all that you can about life and the world around you.

- It is a time to dream big dreams – you can be anything you dream to be, the president of your nation, a scientist, a pilot, scientist, etc. and pray to God to make them come true. The devil knows how important this stage of your life is. Therefore, this is the time he will try to disorganize and confuse your life, if you allow him. For teenagers (guys and girls) the biggest trap Satan sets is in the area of guy/girl relationship. If you are able to escape the guy/girl trap, you can escape any trap in future.

- Recognize that there is time for everything. It is wisest, to leave dating for when you are ready to marry and settle down.

- As a teen the right thing is to relate with boys generally, as ordinary friends, not as lovers and no romance. If you recall, you should have agape and friendship love for all people, but sexual and romantic love must be reserved for marriage.

What must you do to Excel?

It's common these days to read in the papers about the fall in academic standards. But I have also read the story of a girl who made straight As in her senior secondary school certificate exam. My son told me about another girl who has won several spelling bee competitions—she is known as a walking thesaurus. Such achievements do not come on a platter of gold. You must be willing to pay the price for success.

- Determine where you are going in life—make up your mind about what you want to become.

- Set the goals that will help you achieve this dream.

- Avoid distractions. Spend less time in front of the TV, Internet, Whatsapp, and social media.

- You don't have to go to all parties.

- Stay away from friends whose preoccupation is to just gossip and play around.

- Revisit your dream book and study tips on how to develop an eagle vision.

- Create a daily study plan and be committed to it. Give extra time to your weak areas.

- Always be in pursuit of information.

- Save money to go to the cyber cafe if you don't have internet facility at home.

- Ask for help from others e.g. friends, teachers, family.

- Read through your schoolwork every day; don't let it pile,

- Avoid crash programmes.

- Keep ahead of the class/teacher by reading ahead. To do this, you will have to do extra work and research by going to the internet, library, etc.

- Never get involved in exam malpractices.

- Learn all that you can about life and the world around you. Read, read and read some more—readers are leaders.

- Invest in educative resources like books and CDs instead of spending all your money buying makeup kits.

How can you relate with boys and still have clean, pure fun?

All you need is to make up your mind that you want to be an eagle, not a chicken. Know the reason why you want that, because girls and guys who prefer to be chickens will try to influence you to join them. You must determine to influence them to join you rather.

What can boys and girls do together?

1. They can play games, boys versus girls, boy/girl team versus another boy/girl team

2. Read up about countries, hobbies, etc. and discuss them

3. Fashion, cultural, food, etc. shows/exhibitions

4. Sports tournaments/drama/music/dance

5. Debate on various topics

6. Give out topics for each person to research and speak on, award prizes to the best speakers. Examples of topics to speak on:
   → HIV/ AIDS
   → Teenage pregnancy
   → Religion and science
   → Christianity and politics

→   Living a healthy lifestyle

→   Poverty alleviation

7.   Initiate discussions by asking questions, for example:

→   What is the funniest/most embarrassing experience you have ever had?

→   What is the worst or scariest thing that has ever happened to you?

→   What do you like about yourself and why?

→   What would you do if you won 1 million dollars?

→   What will you do if you were president for 24 hours?

→   What is the most painful thing someone said to you?

→   What bad habit have you stopped and how?

→   What do you believe about hell/heaven/the bible?

→   What will you say to someone who doesn't believe in God?

Guys and girls can be so busy having clean fun they won't think of romance or sex. From such healthy friendships true love may blossom at the right time, in its own way.

Note that: One thing you must never forget is, in any guy/girl relationship the girl has the greatest power. A guy will only do what you allow him- unless he is a <u>criminal/rapist!</u>

Helpful guidelines

1.   Think, pray and plan ahead. Tell yourself, 'no matter what he says, no sex, kissing or touching. ', 'if he says this I'll say that'. Today as we go out this is where we should go or this is what we will do. That place and that act are out.' Lord help me to please you.

2. It is wiser and more fun to go out in pairs or a small group. Many more people mean more ideas for fun and opportunities to learn. Above all it helps guard against physical intimacy or sex.

3. Never be alone with a guy in a room, toilet or bathroom, secluded corner or dark place. If you must study together, pray, or talk – do so in an open place, a room with others, a park, etc.

4. It is not wise to ask for or receive expensive gifts from guys– if you do, it weakens your conscience. If they ask for sex or some other favour (Just a kiss) you won't be able to say no. Little things like sweets or a biro pen are okay, but make sure you are not always receiving, you can give too.

5. When a guy begins to touch you in a sexual manner, it's time to speak up and stand up. Say NO! And mean it! If he refuses to back off, begins to fondle you or becomes rude and insulting, it's time to push and walk away!

6. Never tolerate any insult or intimidation from any guy. Look him in the eye and let him know you are a princess and won't accept rotten talk. Let your words, your body language and your eyes all say no. Don't say no when your eyes, tone of voice and body language are saying, '*well, hmmn, maybe!*'

    This may not be easy to do at first, but the more you think of yourself as an eagle and a princess and practice saying what the Bible says you are, your self-image will soar. As yourself image improves, you can boldly look a guy in the eye, and tell him that your no means no, and that's final.

7. Beware of the law of progression–when a guy and a girl spend a lot of time together, the relationship tends towards greater intimacy. They may begin with holding hands, then it's no longer enough, then hugging, (it's getting

sweeter,) then kissing. As time goes on what satisfied them will no longer satisfy, they want more. For example:

Being together--holding hands--simple good night kiss--prolonged kissing--necking--petting--heavy petting--sexual intercourse.

8.   Beware of online dating. Never set up a date with someone you met in an email or chat room. It is impossible to truly know a person or their intentions through a computer. When 16-year-old Mandy turned up for her date she saw he was a grown up man old enough to be her dad! She saw him from afar and took to her heels!

9.   Make sure you have dealt with your IQ.

By her IQ you will know her! The IQ I'm talking about stands for *immodesty quotient*. Immodesty means improper sexual behaviour. A girl with high IQ says by her attitude and the way she carries herself, *"I'm the centre of the universe, available for anyone and everyone, so rub me, hug, kiss, squeeze and pinch any part of me you so desire."* Such a girl is a cheap chicken. She does not know how to control her feelings. By her dressing she invites attention to parts of the body that should be covered. She may even offer sex to guys! (What a shame!) Such a girl will swear that girls are gossips, selfish and full of jealousy, etc. So she prefers to hang out with boys because they are more sincere, kind, etc. But the truth is, she is a chicken. Often such girls get drugged and raped because they would usually be found alone in the company of guys.

One thing girls do not know is this: boys usually say a girl who is an easy catch (cheap chicken), may seem popular alright, but she is often the topic of nasty discussions when the guys are alone. She is seen as a doll (a play-thing). A guy once said she is seen as a 'cooler' where guys go to 'cool off' when "hot" (sexually aroused) others say 'such a girl is like a public towel.'

Discussion Questions

1. What is dating?

2. What are the advantages or disadvantages of dating? Which outweighs the other?

3. What guidelines must a girl follow when dating?

4. In a boy/girl friendship, the girl has the greater power. Discuss.

5. How can girls and boys have fun without sex?

6. What mistakes do girls often make in boy/girl relationships?

7. What should be the focus of the teenage girl?

8. Read Ecclesiastes 3.

Chapter Eleven

Virginity -a priceless Gift

Earlier on we encountered a beauty queen who was a virgin- queen Esther. Who is a virgin? A virgin is a girl or woman who has never had sexual intercourse with a man or boy. At the vaginal opening is a fold of membrane known as the hymen, which is usually broken and causes a little bleeding when a girl has sex for the first time. But the hymen can be broken without sex. It can be broken by inserting objects such as tampons or through sports. The hymen can even be intact after sex. So a girl is still a virgin even if her hymen is broken, provided she has not had sex.

God has given you a wonderful gift, your virginity. Celebrate it! Preserve it for that special man God designed to share your life – your husband. Those girls who say it is old-fashioned to be a virgin are liars. They are jealous and envious of you. They are ashamed to admit their regret and guilt for giving away their most precious gift to a stranger. Don't believe those guys who laugh and try to convince you it is not cool to be a virgin these days. When they are ready to marry, they would go look for a virgin.

Be proud of what you have. Realize that the desires you have to love and be loved in an intimate way are part of God's design. However know that those desires are a sacred, beautiful gift that should be nurtured and allowed to mature and develop within the protective boundaries God has set. Therefore, while you wait, treasure, preserve and be proud of your virginity. God designed you to be a princess, an eagle with holy and high standards. He wants your life to reflect His grace and beauty.

Imagine what would happen today if God wanted to save our great continent-Africa or your town or village through a virgin. He has done it before. He used Mary to birth the saviour of mankind, Christ Jesus. God also used Esther to save Israel from wicked Haman. It was not just her beauty but also her virginity that helped Esther become queen. How many girls (you included) do you know who are determined to be virgins until they get married? Virginity makes a girl attract God's favour. Whenever God wants to use a person He demands that they be consecrated or sanctified. This means to be specially set apart for His use.

'If anyone purifies himself from what is ignoble (immoral), then he will be useful to the master.(2 Timothy 2:20)

God is looking for girls He will use today. He is looking for Marys and Esthers to carry out special assignments for Him. There is so much evil going on in schools, colleges and campuses, and you know it. Rather than allow God to use them many girls prefer to be used of the devil for his wicked, sinful and immoral games. Many are not willing to be virgins.

They prefer to follow the crowd; they don't have the courage to be different. But you are an eagle and can choose today to be different.

Are you a real virgin?

Or do you masturbate, have sex fantasies or have some kind of 'safe sex' where the guy fingers you and 'does not penetrate'? That is not true virginity– It is fake. Virginity is more than just not having sexual intercourse; it's also about purity of the heart and mind. God sees every secret thing, including stuff hidden in our hearts. Many teens fall into the sex trap because they let their mind becomes a junkyard of all kinds of trash. Determine to beautify your mind so that Christ will always feel at home there. How? With songs, Bible verses, dreams of what you want God to do in your life or what you want to do for God. Make your mind the Philippians 4:8 mind, which thinks only of what is pure, lovely, gracious, excellent, and worthy of praise.

Don't lose hope

If you have already made the mistake of giving away your virginity, all hope is not lost. Virginity is a gift you can give to only one person and can only be given once. Once you give it away, you can't get back the outward, physical virginity but you can get back your inner virginity– your purity. This is called secondary virginity. What is secondary virginity? It is to make up your mind that henceforth you will say no to sex until marriage. If you repent, God will forgive you and give you power to begin to live a pure life.

'If we confess our sins He is faithful and just to forgive and cleanse us from all unrighteousness (1John 1:9).'

Physically you are no longer a virgin but God can restore you to become a spiritual virgin. He will not only forgive but also heal you of the wounds of sin. Never believe the lie that once you have tasted sex it is impossible to stop- it is a big lie! Rahab was a prostitute but she repented and God forgave and not only saved her but also used her to save her family *(Joshua chapter 2)* God is a God who gives another chance.

'If any man is in Christ he is a new creation, old things have passed away ... all things have become new.' (2 Corinthians 5:17)

How you can put a stop to premarital-sex:

Use the RRRA!

– **Repent-** Ask God to forgive and cleanse you. Tell the guy (in an open place, never be in a room or secluded place with him again) you have seen your mistake/sin and have repented. Tell him the sexual relationship is over. Stop receiving his calls, delete his no, and stop every visit and contact with him.

- **Renounce-** Ask a godly, mature, trusted woman/pastor to pray and counsel with you. This is extremely important because there are evil spirits involved in sexual sin in particular. A prayer of renunciation may go like this- '*I break every covenant/ connection/soul-tie/emotional-tie with (mention their name[s]). Henceforth I dedicate my body as a temple and vessel of the almighty God. In Jesus name.*"

- **Resist-** Resist every temptation, refuse to think about him, the acts, refuse his calls, invitations. Go out with godly friends, read your Bible, pray, sing praise to God, etc. the devil finds work only for the idle. Pray, '*Satan I resist you in Jesus' name! I bind you unclean spirits in Jesus' name.*' (James 4:6)

- **Accountability-** Tell a trusted godly and mature girl friend to support you in your decision. Call or visit her whenever you are tempted, pray regularly together. The devil will resist your attempt to be free from his bondage, so you need support. It is not easy, but remember -the Lord is your helper (Hebrew13:6).

But I was raped!

Perhaps you did not give away your virginity. It was forcefully taken from you by rape. God can heal you just as He did Joyce Meyer who was raped by her dad many times. I recall the true story of Sandra, who was gang-raped, but later became a motivational speaker and youth Pastor giving hope to many. How did she make it? She had talked to a godly pastor who prayed with her, gave her a Bible to read and counselled with her over a period of time. It was not easy but God helped her.

You too can make it. First, you must stop blaming yourself. Even if you think you caused it, forgive yourself. It is the first step to healing. Then you must forgive whoever raped you. Christ will help you (Philippians 4:13). If you don't, you give the rapist the power to hurt you forever. Another step you must take is to talk to a godly woman you trust and feel okay with about this. You need emotional and spiritual healing. Take that bold step today and discover real freedom, joy and victory!

Past mistakes do not mean one must continue in the same pattern. Don't let your yesterday determine your tomorrow. You can't do anything about yesterday, but you can do everything about today.

Virginity is not a denial of fun, but rather a postponement for the best sex. The best sex occurs when there is a permanent commitment between the partners in marriage. The best sex is when there is no fear, guilt, shame or self-consciousness, which is only possible in marriage.

There are girls who desire to preserve their virginity, but they allow themselves to get entangled in acts that eventually lead them into sex.

Things you must run away from if you truly desire to guard you virginity

(a) <u>Kissing</u>

If you allow a guy to kiss you, you can allow him do anything to you. Such close contact can set your emotions on fire and both of you will end up doing what you had not planned to do. So, save your first kiss for your wedding night.

(b) <u>Don't send or receive letters, text messages, pictures or emails with sexual undertones</u>

These will pollute your mind. The biggest sex organ is not your genitals but your mind. It is in the mind that sex is mixed, cooked and finally served. The enemy of your soul, the devil, knows that if he gets your mind hooked on sex he can control and pull you in any direction he chooses (Proverbs 4:23, Matthew 15:19). When you receive such a message- if you don't know the source, show it to a trusted adult who can counsel and pray with you. If you know the person, confront them personally to stop it or you will report the matter to their parent, pastor, principal, etc. but never take it lightly.

(c) <u>Deep petting</u>

Never undress (partially or completely) before a guy. Never touch a guy or allow him touch you in a sexual manner or fondle each other's genitalia and other areas that can arouse you (erogenous zones) e.g. breast, neck, ear, belly, bum etc. a foolish girl who lacks love and respect for herself will allow a man who is not her husband to touch her body in a sexual way.

The guy might even ask you to let him have sexual release but not by vaginal penetration. The truth is that girls have become pregnant by such foolish and naïve adventures. By the time blood rushes to your erogenous zones and you are on fire with desire, you will be the one begging the guy for sex.

(d) <u>Oral sex</u>

The guy will put his penis in your mouth and ask you to suck. For those of you reading this, who feels nauseated, I'm glad. Once you take sex from God's protective boundary, it becomes ugly, nasty and messy.

(e) <u>Make a pass at a guy</u>

Never tell a guy that you have feelings for him. It shows you are a cheap chicken! Also, if you do, it will arouse both your emotions further. And sooner or later you end up having sex. Actually to tell a guy you have feelings for him is like saying you want to have sex with him. You can control the feeling. Just discipline yourself and determine that you won't cheapen yourself. Avoid the guy. You can also pray for the feeling to go away, it will. If it doesn't, tell a more matured woman, who can guide and counsel you.

When you are surrounded by teen friends who are having sex and seem excited about it, it's not easy if you have chosen to keep your virginity. It is even possible that you are beginning to believe the lie that self-control is not possible. Well I have news for you; self-control is possible, as we will soon see. No matter what others are doing, it's your responsibility to control your God given desires until the appropriate time. The Bible says we must *'Flee the evil desires of youth…'* (2 Timothy 2:22).

Though sex is not evil, when you desire it before marriage, it becomes evil and you must run from it or it will catch and destroy your life.

You Think You Can't Control Yourself?

As earlier said, sweet words and a slight touch can sexually arouse and melt a girl faster than fire melts a candle! However your natural feelings are not meant to control you, you are meant to control them. One of the fruit of the Holy Spirit is self-control (Galatians 5). The Bible says anyone who lacks self-control is like a city that is destroyed because it has no walls to protect it (Proverbs 25:28). But anyone can learn self-control.

Suppose as you are melting in his arms and then suddenly:

* You hear a deafening explosion (like a bomb) the shouts of 'fire! fire'! or

* The ground under your feet begins to tremble and crack or

* The roof caves in!

You think you can't control your feelings?

One way to control your emotions is by self-talk, talk to yourself, e.g.,

'Hey what am I doing? My trousers are being unzipped. He is unbuttoning my blouse; I will soon be naked. I am not a sex tool; I am the temple of God. This kiss is so sweet, but this could be the road to HIV/AIDS and death. No! I must stand up now and push this guy's hand away before we go too far. This is not love; he just wants to use my body. It is not right; after this I will hate myself for being cheap.'

What I am saying is that, if you desire, you have the ability to stop yourself and the guy. Shout *'No! Stop this, it's a sin'*. Push his hand away and stand up. Walk away from him and dress up. Your heart may be pounding and you may feel as if you are about to faint, but you will be okay. Most guys will stop, not all men are rapists. God trusts you at this point to make the right decision; He will help you. According to the Bible, one practical and wise step is to flee (2 Timothy 2: 22)*'Flee the evil desires of youth.'*

If you refuse to take the responsibility, you are like the person described in Proverbs 6:27 who walks on and carries hot coals with their bare hands and expects not to be burnt.

Discussion Questions

1. Who is a virgin?

2. What is the importance of keeping your virginity? Read Genesis 2:24.

3. Why are so many girls giving it away? Read 1 Corinthians 6:12-20.

4. Virginity is not just physical; it begins in the mind. Discuss.

5. What is secondary virginity?

6. To keep your virginity, what must you run from?

7. How can a girl learn self-control? Read Genesis 39:7

Chapter Twelve

Eagles and their Parents

Even though Riska was from a humble background, she was a bright and intelligent girl. Her parents, hardworking farmer (dad) and fruit-seller (mom) adored her. Their joy knew no bounds when she won a scholarship to a prestigious school. On a certain visiting day, her mum had gone to visit her. While most parents arrived in shiny posh cars, she arrived with dusty feet and a basket of food and fruits for her dear daughter. She sat under a mango tree and sent for Riska.

Guess what Riska's response was?

"My mum? That's not my mum!" Riska protested. "Perhaps it's the nanny or cook," she lied. At the end it was an embarrassing and sad story for everyone. The reality is that our parents may not meet up with our expectations yet they are still our parents. To be ashamed of or deny them, is to be ashamed of and a denial of ourselves. Riska should have showed off her mum to her friends. 'Hey girls come meet the coolest mum on planet earth!' None of us chose our parents, God did. It is through them that God gave us life. Therefore just as we want others to accept and love us with all our faults, we must equally learn to accept and love our parents.

Some things your parents wish you to know:

1. They love you and desire the best for you.
2. Many times they do not know how to communicate this love.

3. They never went to school to learn how to be parents, so they make many mistakes.

4. They desire that your life be better than theirs.

5. Their desire to see you succeed may often make them seem hard and at times wicked.

6. They are discouraged when they are not able to give you the best they desire.

7. They are human beings with personal issues/problems.

8. Some of them suffer from the effects of their childhood background e.g., anger, shame, sexual abuse, poverty, inadequate education, etc.

9. They have regrets and disappointments with life.

10. As they age, many develop health problems, like diabetes, high-blood pressure, heart problems, etc.

11. Some may be divorced and single, and this affects them emotionally and physically, e.g. sleepless nights.

12. Their business or job may not be doing well enough, so it affects them.

13. Sometimes they struggle with their faith; they feel God has forsaken them.

Why do you need to know all these? So that you may better understand your parents and so be able to relate better with them, especially your moms. Parents differ just as teens differ. As you don't like your parents comparing you with others, neither should you compare your parents with other parents. People's backgrounds, personalities, needs, weaknesses and strengths differ.

You must realise that your mum is a gift from God to you. She is there as your guide, mentor, pastor, teacher and friend. No doubt, some mothers may seem like they are agents of Satan, and will need God's intervention in their own lives. But most mothers dearly love and desire the best for their daughters. For this reason, the devil constantly attacks and tries to interfere with your relationship with your mother. He wants to destroy the mother-daughter bond. He wants to convince you she is a bad woman or a witch, but Satan is a liar. Lola, a nineteen year old girl was convinced her mum hated her, so she ran away from home, only to end up as a prostitute and later contracting AIDS. That is Satan's plan. He is a crafty destroyer, who recognizes the great importance of the relationship between a mum and her daughter.

"Be self-controlled and alert, your enemy the devil prowls around like a roaring lion looking for someone to destroy" (1 Peter 5:8).

What you need is to be humble and patient with your mum and to learn to pray always. As you pray, God will give you wisdom and grace to overcome.

How should we treat our Parents?

The Bible gives us clear simple guidelines (Proverbs 3:1-2, Ephesians 6:1-2).

My son, do not forget my teaching, but keep my commands in your heart, for they will prolong your life many years and bring you prosperity.

'Children obey your parents in the Lord for this is right Honour your father and mother —which is the first commandment with a promise,-that it may go well with you and that you may enjoy long life on earth.'

Obedience and honour

These are two gifts to give our parents. If you were a parent how would you want your kids to treat you?

Some practical ways to honour your parents (guardians/adult in your life)

1. **Respect**. Treat them with respect e.g. don't sit while they stand, except when they want it so. Never you talk back at them or be rude or insulting. Apologize sincerely when you hurt them.

2. **Serve them**. Help set the table, clear and wash up after meals- offer to do so even when there is a domestic help to do it. Especially do something personal for them e.g. make a cup of tea, serve them their meal, iron or wash for them, clean their shoes etc.

3. **Remember special occasions**, e.g. birthdays and anniversaries. Bake a cake, make a fancy birthday or anniversary card, buy a cheap simple gift or write them a poem or a note of appreciation.

4. **Pray for them** – ask for their prayer concerns.

5. **Obey them** and submit to their authority.

6. **Save money and take them out** (it does not have to be expensive). They will never forget it all their lives.

7. **Give compliments** e.g. 'You look nice, you are a good cook,' 'you are a kind dad', etc.

8. **Express gratitude**. 'Thank you for paying my fees', 'for being there for me', 'for loving me enough to correct me,' etc.

9. **Communicate**. Make an effort to confide in them about school, friends, your faith, struggles, etc. It pains them when you keep them out of issues in your life. Ask them questions to know what is happening in their lives.

10. **Unconditional love**. Parents are human beings; they are not perfect, so are prone to many mistakes. Determine to love them no matter your disappointments with them.

Even though the Bible commands us to be good to our parents and other adults in our life, I am well aware that it is not always easy. Parents and guardians can at times be quite difficult to handle. So what do you do? Let's find out.

When Parents and other adults are difficult

Here are some real life stories: 16-year-old Prisca's mum shares with Prisca stories of escapades with boyfriends when she was young. A mum I know smokes and drinks alcohol in the presence of her daughter and complains by saying things like, "Men are useless." Yet she complains when her 16-year-old girl trades insults with her and refuses to help her with chores.

Why do parents sometimes behave the way they do? Why would a mom call her own daughter a prostitute? Why will a mother encourage her daughter to sleep with men for money? Why do some parents sometimes harm their own children? Loretta a 15-year-old had refused to heed the mom's instruction to cook a meal. Yet after the mom finished the cooking, she went to help herself to some of the food. So out of provocation her mom hit her on the head with a stick and the girl fell down and died (the devil worked overtime there!).

As mentioned earlier, your parents are human, therefore they are not perfect. We do not excuse some bad things parents do. However as earlier mentioned, some of the things we said they wished you knew would help you understand and better deal with some of their weird behaviour. Teens are at a phase of life where parents need to take time to understand them. Teens also need to be patient with their parents because understanding teens is not an easy job. It takes the love and wisdom of God to bring up children. Many of our parents do not have a personal relationship with Christ, so they are not able to tap God's resources that would have helped them in their role as parents. Even some who are committed

Christians may not know how to tap the wisdom and grace of God for their roles as parents.

One of the best true life stories that I know is that of Dr. Phil, a famous and successful American psychologist. As he grew up his dad was an alcoholic who spent most of his money on alcohol leaving his family hungry. Phil would deliver newspapers to make money to feed the family as a teenager of about 15. Many nights he had to go out to go look for his dad. He would find him slumped in a gutter. This teen would search his dad's pockets for the car keys and drive his dad home in the middle of the night, even though he had no driving license because he was under 18. Though he hated his dad's lifestyle, he kept treating him with respect. Most of all he made up his mind that he will never be like his dad. But his sisters were not as determined as he was. They let their dad's lifestyle influence them negatively. So they ended up living wayward lives.

Earlier on we saw the case of Joyce Meyer who was even sexually abused by her dad, but she forgave him, led him to a saving faith in Christ and baptized him in water. No matter how problematic our parents are, with God's help we can overcome. As earlier said, eagles are never intimidated by storms; rather they are able to soar right through and above storms with their powerful wings. Sometimes when the situation seems more than we can handle we can seek prayers and counsel from matured godly people, like a pastor, teacher, woman of God, etc. Whatever the case, let's never give up on our parents or hate them.

For dads and other male relatives

This is a personal cry from my heart. I want you to realize that God has deposited awesome power on a man. It can be described as the anointing of manhood, or of leadership. It is the God given grace bestowed on men to be strong, to guide, shield and protect.

However because of what the devil did at the fall of man, many men do not understand how to use this power. In addition to what the devil did, cultures and traditions of men have further corrupted this power. The result being that manhood is often seen as aggression, hardness, aloofness, insensitivity, and often, cruelty.

In a particular African nation, research indicates that 40% of sexual abuse on girls was done by their own dads. How tragic!

You must realize that the perception a girl has about her dad goes a long way in shaping the kind of woman she becomes and the way she relates with the world around her. The girl child is a gift from God to this world, especially the African continent. The future of our nation and continent depends on the well being of the girl child. She is the mother of tomorrow; she shapes the destiny of civilization. The potentials, spiritually, economically and otherwise of the girl child can only be imagined. Yet statistics show that the African girl child is grossly neglected, often abused and brutalized by the very person she looks up to for her well being and protection. It is sad that laws need to be made by international bodies to safeguard the welfare of the girl child. This is why I saw it necessary to add this chapter to this book. Perhaps a dad will pick it up out of curiosity and read it when no one is watching!

For the men who are already playing their role well, may this serve as an inspiration to the indispensable role you are called to play in a girl's life.

What you mean in the life of your daughter.

1. You help her develop a healthy self-image. A girl's self image determines how she lives her life and the choices she makes; because a person is controlled by the way they see themselves. Girls who are loved, appreciated by and are close to their dads tend to feel great about themselves and are often more self confident. As a dad or daddy

figure, determine to show interest in your girl(s) academics, her joys and pains, buy small gifts, joke with her, hug her and take her out for walks or on a date, etc.

2. You present her with a picture of God the father.

    A girl, who is often criticized, shouted at, cruelly treated by her own father will find it difficult to connect with a heavenly father who is love. If a girl cannot relate with a loving earthly father, she finds it difficult to relate with an invisible heavenly one. But if she has a truly loving dad/male figure she likely will enjoy a deep loving relationship with her heavenly dad.

3. You give her a picture of what men are.

    It is from you that your daughter picks up her first and significant view of what men are like. If you are kind, caring and supportive she tends to believe men are like that and will plan to choose a man like you to marry. If you are distant, absent and abusive she equally will feel all men are like that. This may likely lead to her going through her teen and young adult life looking for the love and protection you never gave. And she will go from one sugar daddy to another; from man to man searching for love. Eventually in desperation to meet her emotional needs, she may end up marrying the wrong kind of man because she never had a true picture of one.

4. Her overall physiological well being is dependent on you.

    Science has proved that girls who do not have a close relationship with their dads tend to start their menses at an abnormally earlier age.

5. One of the greatest investments you can make in your daughter's life or that of any girl-child is to teach her about man/woman relationship from a man's perspective. She needs to hear from you the fact that many men

think about sex in unhealthy, unbiblical and selfish ways. Above all she needs to hear you lovingly but firmly point her towards what is true, biblical and pleasing to God. She needs to see a man who she can trust with her femininity.

Discussion Questions

1. Why must teens appreciate and accept their parents?

2. How should teens appreciate their parents and guardians?

3. What could make parents to often seem harsh and wicked to their teens?

4. Why do you think girls and their mums are often at loggerheads?

5. What can a teenage girl do to improve her relationship with her mum?

6. What should be a teen's attitude towards difficult parents or guardians?

7. Would you pray that your own children relate with you the way you are presently relating to your parents? Explain your response.

Chapter Thirteen

Girl, it is worth it!

As I begin to draw the curtains on this great adventure, my advice to you dear girl is: Guard Your Heart. This is God's word to you. 'Guard *your heart with all diligence for out of it is the well spring of life*' (Proverbs 4:23). Why would God say that we should guard it above all else? The reason we should guard our heart more than anything is because our life-character, values, dreams and choices flow out of our heart. Your heart is the real you. During the teen/adolescent phase, a girl's heart is quite vulnerable/fragile. Just like the petals of a beautiful flower it can be easily crushed, especially by those who do not value it's worth and beauty. During the adolescent stage, a girl's heart is easy target for negative and dangerous influence.

Be a Woman of Character

It is not easy to say no, but once you take that first bold step, you are on your way to becoming a woman of confidence and character. You determine your own character, it's your choice. No one can make you become what you don't want to be. Eagles never compromise. Rather it is their character to soar above the storm. You too with God's help can develop the strength and courage to soar above all the challenges that confront you. Boldness and courage does not mean you are not afraid, but that you refuse to surrender to fear. Character is not a gift– but it is developed and built in the midst of difficult situations, over a long period of time. As you make daily, difficult but wise choices, you are on your way to becoming a woman of character. A woman that will attract the best of men not vagabonds.

How do you recognize a woman of character? A woman of character has a high MQ & SRQ!

A girl's MQ is her *modesty quotient* – to be modest is to dress and act in a way that does not arouse or attract the opposite sex. Such a girl has a positive self-image and high self esteem. She does not need to use her God-given beauty and curves to make herself the centre of attraction. But then, she is also not a weird 'spirito' who talks only of God and the Bible. She is also practical and down to earth, friendly and is interested in the well being of others.

The SRQ is the *self-respect quotient*. A girl with a high MQ naturally has a high SRQ. She respects herself, for she recognizes she is made in God's image. She has a purpose and vision for her life. She is an eagle. Even if she falls in love, she does not throw away her common sense. She exercises self-control over her emotions. She has great aspirations and dreams for her future, which she won't risk for temporary pleasure.

'Do you not know that in a race all the runners run, but only one gets the prize? Run in such a way as to get the prize.' (1 Corinthians 9:27)

So I challenge you to **Desire, Decide, Determine** and **Dare** to be more than just a girl-be an eagle. There are too many defeated chicken girls out there. They are waiting for an eagle like you to show them how to soar. How cool it would be if you choose to be that eagle!

The teen years can be fun and exciting, but like we have seen, full of danger as well. This is why we need other people to help us along the way. The Bible says that two are better than one and iron sharpens iron. How can this help? By having what I call your dream team (DT).

Your dream team (DT)

Have you looked for, prayed for and developed your dream team? These are people you know who love and fear God and are purpose-driven. In addition, they love you and care enough to help you become the woman God made you to be. They will still love you even when you fall. But they will help you get up and stay on your feet. They are not afraid to tell you the truth, even if it hurts.

Who can be on your DT?

Your mother (sometimes this may not apply, if your mom is late, immoral or you live with someone else). God will bring a godly woman to help you.

Friends who love God and desire to grow and are growing. It's better to have more girls on your DT. You can share anything with them, pray, study and talk deeply. Too much closeness with guys can lead to sexual intimacy.

Others you may have on your team:

Sunday school teacher, youth leader, school teacher, aunt, female pastor, step-mom etc.

Tell whomever you choose, "I want to discuss with you once in a while about my struggles as a teen. I'll be honest and open and I'd like you to guide, rebuke, correct and pray with me and for me." The person should also be free to call you from time to ask how you are doing.

Attention mothers!

Nurturing and bringing up a girl is one of the most frustrating and challenging (scary!) yet fulfilling experiences any mother could ask for. But how do you overcome the formidable challenges and reap the thrill of victory and fulfilment at the end of your labours (and battles!)? This is how:

→   Be a praying mother. Prayer releases the divine wisdom, grace and power a mother needs to guide and teach a girl to become a woman after God's heart- a woman of virtue and excellence.

→   Know, speak, pray the Word of God- it arms you with the weapon you need to fight and win the battle for your daughter's destiny and soul.

→   Be a mentor not a monster- if you are approachable, friendly and positive in your attitude to issues, it grants you access into your daughter's heart. If you act as a judge or terrorist you harden her heart and widen the gap between you two.

→   Be sincere - let your daughter know you also had struggles and made mistakes as a young girl. Show her how you overcame.

→   Be humble and vulnerable- admit to your daughter that you don't have all the answers.

→   Apologize when you offend or hurt her. Ask for her prayers and opinion. Find out what she thinks about you and your methods/style.

You think all these will weaken your authority and render you ineffective? On the contrary, it will disarm the devil and create a conducive atmosphere for the Holy Spirit to work, and above all, grant you an expressway into your daughter's heart.

A mother I know who is very negative, critical and abusive says to her teen daughter "Men are rogues and insincere, keep away from them!" The girl does not trust or believe her and sleeps around with boys and men.

The Bible records, *'For the foolishness of God is wiser than man's wisdom, and the weakness of God is stronger than man's strength.'* (1 Corinthians 1: 25)

You have read all these and you wonder: 'How can I become an eagle?'

Say this prayer and mean it with all your heart:

Lord Jesus, I am a sinner, I have lived like a chicken, forgive me. I believe that you died and rose again from the dead for my sins. Please come into my heart and wash away my sins. Give me the power to become a child of God and to begin from today to soar like an eagle. Thank you for answering me. Amen.

The Purity Covenant

Lord Jesus, I confess that I have treated this body as if it is mine to do with as I please. I ask you to forgive me. I hereby dedicate my spirit, soul and body to you for your use. Let your Spirit rule and use my life. Give me the grace to keep myself pure from now until I get married and to keep myself for that man you will want me to marry one of these days. I promise to stay a virgin until my wedding day. Help me to resist every power or influence that wants me to break this covenant.

Name _____

Signature _____

Date _____

Witness _____

Discussion Questions

1. Why must you guard your heart?

2. Whose responsibility is it to determine your character?

3. Who is a woman of character & how do you recognise her?

4. How is character developed?

5. Who is in your dream team? What qualities should you seek in your dream team?

6. If you don't have a dream team when will you develop one?

7. To whom does your body belong? What agreement have you made with God about your body?

Reading List

1. *Acts Magazine*, International Edition, vol.37, No 1, pg. 46.

2. *Best Friends For Life* by Michael and Judy Philips, Bethany House Publishers 1997, Minneapolis, Minnesota.

3. A.C. Greene, *Game Plan Abstinence Program* by Scott Phelps and Libby Gray, 20d Project Reality.

4. *New Life Style to Adolescent and Parents,* Dr Julian Melgoss.

5. *I Don't Want Your Sex for Now* by Miles McPherson, Bethany House, Bethany Press International, Bloomington Minnesota, 2001.

6. *Love & Marriage* by Bruce & Carol Britten, Worldwide Books.

About The Author

Irene Nndali Isiguzo is a missionary with Calvary Ministries (CAPRO)- an International, inter-denominational, indigenous Missions Agency whose headquarters are in Nigeria. She and her husband, Chi, have been missionaries for over 20 years. They were cross-cultural missionary trainers for seven years in Kenya. They are currently serving as disciple-makers and also involved with various aspects of missions in South Africa.

Irene holds a Bachelor of Science Degree in Education. She is also an alumnus of the Leadership Training Institute and Haggai Leadership Institute in Nairobi.

Irene and Chi are blessed of God with many children. The biological ones are Joshua, Shalom and David. Irene has a passion to empower the youth of today to become "defiant in their stand for Christ." She seeks ways to equip young ladies to become women of virtue and excellence.